SUPER ACHIEVERS

THE
TEN PROVEN PRINCIPLES
OF SUCCESS

Sean P. McCullough
with Rick Young, PhD

Forward By
BEN GAY III

authorHOUSE®

AuthorHouse™
1663 Liberty Drive
Bloomington, IN 47403
www.authorhouse.com
Phone: 1 (800) 839-8640

Photo of Sean P. McCullough from author's collection
Photo of Rick Young by R. P. Allen

Published by AuthorHouse 03/11/2019

ISBN: 978-1-7283-0341-3 (sc)
ISBN: 978-1-7283-0340-6 (e)

Library of Congress Control Number: 2019902726

Print information available on the last page.

This book is printed on acid-free paper.

DEDICATION

This book is dedicated to my parents Patrick and Eileen McCullough. To my wife Karen and three children Austin, Amber and Carolyn. And to ALL the aspiring entrepreneurs finding their sweet spot in serving and helping others with their products, services, gifts, talents, and abilities.

—Sean P. McCullough

To my grandchildren: Brandon and Brianna Michelle; Joseph, Brianna Lynn, and Cristina.
May you each find your own joy of success in life!

—Rick Young

CONTENTS

PREFACE

There are numerous books out on the issue of obtaining success. Many of them are true, accurate, and extremely helpful. Many of them are written by men and women who have been so successful that one would want to start, and probably end, with them alone.

So, why write a book on the subject of success when there already is such a crowded field? The answer is simple: We are writing especially for the young adult. Someone who may be intimidated by what they view as a "complicated" reading, because the author of those other books is *so* successful.

That is not to say *we* have not been successful. On the contrary. But, we have a heart for the relatively "young" person who is willing to take on the challenges of starting a business... or any enterprise for that matter, and, even, in some cases, the individual "starting over." For that reason, we have written accordingly.

For the high school senior, starting over as he or she enters a new college; for the college senior, starting over in a new career born of that recent college diploma; for the military veteran, starting over in an attempt to springboard their armed forces experience into a civilian profession, this book is for you.

We have intentionally written this as a primer, an introduction, to the elements of character necessary to succeed. It is our hope that the reader will progress to the more "advanced" books written by some of the most successful persons in the business, sales, and other professional industries. Many of the men and women who have been interviewed in our book, have writings of their own. We encourage you to seek them out to increase your knowledge of the principles that will lead to *your* personal success.

Finally, and unashamedly, we acknowledge our own Christian faith that, we feel, is *the* basis of success. Every single one of the proven principles of success presented here are grounded in Scripture. Whatever your own personal belief system, the books of Proverbs and Ecclesiastes, amongst others, are age-old guides, because many of their principles are found in the secular writings of others, whether ancient or more modern.

For the many reasons presented here, we hope you enjoy – and employ – the wisdom that you are about to read.

Sean P. McCullough
Havertown, Pa

Rick Young
Howell, NJ

FOREWORD

I have known Sean P. McCullough since 2013 when he attended a CEO Space International Class where I was a keynote speaker. It is safe to say we hit if off like peas and carrots at a Sunday dinner.

As a successful entrepreneur in sales and motivational speaking for over five decades, I look forward to each of my speaking engagements to meet and identify participants who I know have what it takes to be successful themselves. Sean is one of those special people!

This book, *Super Achievers: The Ten Proven Principles of Success*, written by Sean, is a confirmation of what I saw in him at that CEO Space International gathering. And its contents confirm Sean's deep desire to help others achieve the success they are meant to have… if these ten principles become a part of not only their business life, but also their everyday life.

Super Achievers: The Ten Proven Principles of Success has been written for those who are just beginning to explore striking out on their own for the first time: The high school or college student who has heard that deep heartfelt call to create his or her own business, be a meaningful contribution to a business already in existence, or simply to branch out on one's own. But, you don't have to be a young man or woman to find this book insightful… you just need to be young at heart in your desire to walk the path of success.

To accomplish this, Sean's book provides a style that should speak directly to any audience. It is built on the testimonies of very successful people. It lets the reader learn how that success was achieved: Who they are. What they have accomplished. Why they began on their own. Where and when many of them began. How many of them were led to begin and become successful. You will also read of their trials and tribulations, something that will be faced by all who have the courage to make the attempt.

Sean has let each of these people speak for themselves in order for you to better understand the process that leads to success. It is his hope you will be able to "translate" these testimonies into your own life and entrepreneurial, or other venture, undertaking.

You should listen to the witnessing of each of these successful people. You will find in your reading that the pathway to your own success is contained in each of these personal testimonies. As you read, you will find things that excite your own desire for success. And you will identify methods that resonate with you… things that you know, deep down inside, will lead to your own success.

There are, of course, many books on the market about how to achieve success. What makes *Super Achievers: The Ten Proven Principles of Success* so unique as a guide for a person to achieve the desires of their heart lies in the background of co-author Rick Young.

Rick is a combat veteran of the Vietnam War and author of *Combat Police: U.S. Army Military Police in Vietnam.* He has added a touch to the narrative that should speak clearly to returning veterans who, themselves, are looking to start something of their own.

The book, then, speaks to these men and women who want to use their learned discipline and experienced military skills to not only begin their own enterprise, but to enrich the nation they so willingly and competently served. This book will be a sure guide as you work towards that post-military success.

With this book in hand, enjoy your journey!

Ben Gay III
Placerville, CA
www.BFG3.com

Author, *The Closers-Part1, The Closers-Part 2, The Closers-Part 3, Sales Closing Power!*

ACKNOWLEDGEMENTS

The authors wish to express their profound thanks to those who have significantly contributed to this writing. This includes all those very successful individuals who took time from their busy schedules to provide their honest – and heartfelt – interviews. This includes (alphabetically), Chris Cayer, Lane Etheridge, Stephanie Frank, Ben Gay III, Bob Holmes, Paul Hoyt, Eric Lofholm, Ken MacArthur, Dr. Jeff McGee, Dr. Will Moreland, Jessica Peterson, Ken Rochon, Chris Salem, Dr. Len Schwartz, Robert "Bob" Salomon, Jim Vaughn, and coach Andre M. "A.M." Williams. You all are indeed the heart and soul of this book!

A special thank you to Ben Gay III, for taking the time to provide the Forward.

We also want to especially thank Gloria Hass for her tireless effort, and countless hours, in transcribing all the interviews to make this book a reality.

Finally, and most of all, we want to thank our spouses, Karen Kempski McCullough and Linda Young, for their never-ending support and, especially, their sacrifice of innumerable hours granted to us in the book's preparation.

We thank all of you for making this book come to life.

Introduction

In 1927, American writer Max Ehrmann (1872–1945) wrote the prose poem *Desiderata*, a Latin word meaning *desired things*. Remaining largely unknown in the author's lifetime, the text became widely celebrated after its use in devotional and spoken-word recordings in the early 1970s.

In the poem Ehrmann penned:

> Keep interested in your own career, however humble;
> it is a real possession in the changing fortunes of time.

The impact a person's career has, can be seen early-on in first-meeting introductions. There, one's occupation is often stated somewhere in the first three sentences or, the result of the first three questions. *What do you do for a living*? often masks the unspoken question: How *successful* are you?

It is the intent in the writing of this book to guide you towards answering both those questions by stating your very own success. To accomplish this requires considering Ehrmann's further *Desiderata* advice:

> Be yourself…. [yet] take kindly the counsel
> of the years…

To draw from the "council of the years," there are presented herein the experiences of numerous *very* successful people. In this way you do not have to invest years yourself, but can glean from them *in minutes* the principles necessary to succeed.

Lastly, there is Ehrmann's observation on life itself:

> You are a child of the universe,
> no less than the trees and the stars;
> you have a right to be here.
> And whether or not it is clear to you,
> no doubt the universe is unfolding as it should.

You *are* a child of the universe and you *do* have a right to be here. But there is more: Every person who has ever walked this planet, anyone who is in possession of a relatively sound mind, should know he or she has a unique calling and purpose placed on the life they have been given.

This calling is something that can only be accomplished *by them*. For that reason, it is often referred to as the "Divine Calling & Purpose." Each person, then, has been given the opportunity to succeed at that purpose, the one for which they have been called.

This book is to help you find – and work towards – that success.

1   ORIGINS

It is our attitude at the beginning of a difficult task which,
more than anything else, will affect its successful outcome.

William James

or-i-gin *n.* the point at which someone
or something starts: BEGINNING.

The cliché "every journey begins with the first step" holds
as true today as when it was first coined. The inverse holds
equally as true: *no* journey begins *without* the first step. The
amount of people who have thought about an undertaking, but
have done nothing more, is too innumerable to count; totaling
every grain of sand on all the seashores.

But, for each person who has gone on to be an unqualified
success, there is *always* that first step taken towards that
success. This is what separates the daydreamer from the doer.
And, there is not one successful person who cannot reach back
into his or her past and clearly identify the beginnings that
would lead to that success.

As you read the origins of the successful people presented here,
reflect on your own past. You are encouraged to look upon

those people and events you've previously encountered – and even those of today – which have been, or are, inexorably working on you to guide you towards your own success.

One of the finest examples is that of Stephanie Frank.

Stephanie Frank is an international performance coach, behaviorist, and cyber intelligence expert. Among her many accomplishments, she made her first million dollars by the age of 22. So, it is with tongue-in-cheek she has authored the international bestselling book, *The "Accidental" Millionaire*.

Stephanie is expert in helping people master their lives so that they can better enjoy their time, money, laughter and love; the things for which virtually all are looking. She has helped thousands of individuals and organizations around the world be more efficient, productive, and streamlined so that they can get more out of what they want – and do so faster than ever before.

Guided by her time-tested principles, Stephanie's clients can quickly go from local, one-person proprietorships to global, multiple-employee, million-dollar operations through her techniques that lead to mastery of the Internet. She has built her own current customer base to over 43,000 people in 85 countries using these same exact strategies and thinking habits that she teaches.

Like all those who are successful, Stephanie can relate to her beginnings being linked with her early education. She relates that even as a child she had "a really, really strong 'why.' " It stemmed from her educational years. Yet, even today she asks that question a lot to each situation she faces: "Why am I…?"

Regarding that early education, she notes she was a good student when she wanted to be a good student. That generally showed up in topics or subjects that she liked, or topics and subjects that she understood *why* she might need to know them in the future. But for the courses she didn't enjoy, like social studies or geography, she questioned, *why* bother at all?

This made her a kind of rebel, the way she would question the need for taking certain courses. And it was not an acceptable way of thinking back then in traditional school. Nonetheless, she was a solid B-plus, A-minus student.

But, she felt bad for her parents who had to drag themselves to the parent-teacher conferences where they were forever told, "Stephanie is such a great thinker. She's very, very smart. I don't know why she just can't get all A's." Her parents would say, "Because she's bored!"

And, indeed, she *was* bored. What she really needed was more *worthwhile* information to consume. As an example, she often completed her homework while she was in class; rarely doing it at home – because she quickly grasped the concept being taught. Unfortunately, this led many to think she was cocky. Or some maybe thought she was lazy.

The truth was, she just wanted to get her homework done so she could go and then explore things she thought worthwhile. Things that she really wanted to learn about. Things like nature or science or math or fashion design. She was this way all the way through school, especially high school.

High school, however, would not be a total loss for her. Stephanie would become aware that even a negative encounter could produce results for a person with desires to succeed.

There were two defining instances in high school that would guide her and define her on-going motivation. Both of them spoke directly to her because they impacted her search for the *why*.

It is this search that speaks directly to her core value of *freedom*. In answering the *why* of anything, which she has done throughout her entire life, she is searching: Will her actions make her free or will they ensnare her? She most definitely does not want to be a captive in a box!

In high school she had a math teacher, a rough-and-tumble, gruff kind of a guy, who used to think she was just cocky. This was probably because she loved the basics of math. The teacher would write a problem on the board – advanced algebra – and Stephanie quickly understood it; to a point where she had an immediate answer. The problem was, she couldn't comprehend how she arrived at her answer.

That is when the teacher accused her of cheating. This occurred again-and-again, pretty much throughout her entire time in his math class.

That wrongful accusation, however, was a really defining moment for her. She realized she was perceived as someone that she knew she wasn't; she was *not* a cheat… nor a liar. But, she did realize she was different.

The huge, life-illuminating impact for Stephanie was, "Wait a minute. It's done. It's correct. Who cares if I've done it exactly the way they think it should be done?" The math teacher was confining her. She had answered the *why* differently, but had come up with the correct answer.

That realization brought a sense of freedom.

The second defining moment for Stephanie in high school would be an insight into "attitude adjustment."

It came in geography class. There she struggled, really *struggled*, with geography. Homework for geography was done at home! Because she just didn't get it. It was the direct opposite of math, where she could work intuitively.

The struggle led to mental pain: What is a continent? Where is Antarctica? Where is this or that? ("Who cares"?!!?)

As a successful business woman, Stephanie views our education system as being built on a 16th century model; one that was meant to make good soldiers: Sit down, follow the rules, do what we tell you to do. Yet, people today, especially those of the Millennial generation, are the opposite of that. It's not celebrated in school that you go with your strengths. It's celebrated that you have the correct response to a well-rounded education.

She clearly remembers very distinctly being in her sophomore year and her mother was helping her with geography homework. "Pretty much unsuccessfully," she adds. "I finally remember looking at her, 'You know what? I know that eventually I have to understand all this. I don't understand why right now. But one day I'm just going to travel the world. Maybe then I can figure it out by *doing* geography along the way.'"

She now admits that might sound flippant. At that moment though, Stephanie remembers she again was looking towards that "why." *Why* did it give her freedom to understand what the world looks like?

And the answer?

> "I have now been all over the world and my geography has become the back of an American Airlines' magazine. I actually have it pinned up in my office along with the American Airlines' world map with all their plane routes. I have pegged on that map all the places that I've been to; all those different countries and continents that I just couldn't understand when I was in geography.

> "Because I projected the possible need into the future, if I ever did travel, I would need to know geography. I forced myself to learn it back then. I was answering the 'why,' because I had changed my point of view. I had had an attitude adjustment!"

As you can see from Stephanie's description of her origins, her greatest initial impacts were in high school. This leads to an observation that is often overlooked: a college experience – or degree – is not necessarily a must to be successful.

But it is helpful to have a love of learning. Just ask Ken Rochon.

Ken is an international author and speaker. He is considered an expert in branding and social media, as well as viral marketing with events all over the world. He enjoys implementing and studying strategies that leveraging, like-minded and light-hearted audiences want, in order to create epic, social-proof campaigns for his clients.

As an expert in his field, Ken is invited to some of the largest international events and speaks on the biggest stages regarding how to collaborate and orchestrate influence to cause social-proof viral campaigns. These campaigns benefit the host, the sponsors, the speakers, and everyone attending the event.

Ken has authored over 17 books on multiple topics including children linguistics, marketing, networking and travel. His current book is called *Keep Smiling, Shift Happens.* This book has caused the movement of celebrities and leaders to want to join, helping remind the world that positivity attracts positive power.

Further, Ken is considered a humanitarian and a philanthropist for he does hundreds of events in which his company volunteers to support and market each year.

His desire is inspiring – living a purpose-driven life – which has caused him to create his company called "The Umbrella Syndicate." This organization supports authors, leaders and speakers. Ken's ability to see the vision of a leader and cause the perception of the vision to become a reality is one of the reasons he is included in so many amazing concept conventions and projects.

One of the things that Ken really loves is traveling. He's accomplished one of his bucket list items by visiting over one hundred of the world's countries.

All of this success stems from his origins.

Ken recalls his entire schooling was really an extension of his family's input. They constantly fed him knowledge through love. At the same time, they fed him love through knowledge. They found out what he wanted to learn and then gave him books on those topics.

"For instance," he recalls, "my Uncle Bob gave me a book when I was probably five years old on how to draw horses. From that positive exposure to drawing, I ended up going into college with a five-year focus on medical illustration, as well as a focus on science and art."

Another uncle, when he was 18, gave him a book called *The E-myth* by Michael Gerber. Ken notes that Gerber has influenced millions of people over these many decades. So, Ken holds this as one of the most important books an entrepreneur can read. It's about the entrepreneurial myth and why so many businesses go out of business. Michael Gerber then shows what you can do to prevent that from happening to your business.

Notwithstanding his desire to learn, Ken admits he was hyperactive and probably unmanageable as a student. Not in every class, but in those classes where the teacher didn't really engage him. He thinks that if his teachers were asked, they probably considered him not a very great student.

But, he considers himself in good company. He observes, Einstein was considered a horrible student too.

From his perspective, now as an adult, Ken thinks he was possibly average. He admits he mostly did the bare minimum to pass, and made sure he didn't do anything in school that would get him into trouble at home.

From the teacher, however, who really taught in his learning style, he actually learned. Like most hyperactive students, he was typically bored. He really needed the subject matter to engage him on a higher level. Then he *loved* learning!

He credits that desire to learn from his mom, his grandmother, and even his father. The enjoyment of reading or the enjoyment of new ideas and how the world works, he was just fascinated by it.

So, he was a bad student, as they say, "on paper," i.e., in teacher evaluations. But he was awesome when it came to learning the stuff that interested him. He notes he honestly had a real thirst for learning. For that reason, he related to teachers who pushed him.

Ken reflected on teachers who did just that.

> "In fifth grade, I had a science teacher, Mr. Ingle. He was an extremely tough teacher. I didn't do that well in his class, in part because I feared him. He was very strict. Not from a mean standpoint, but from a standpoint that his curriculum of fifth grade science was taught at a level of high school. So, I feared him, because I feared the challenge he brought to the class. I fought to get a grade of C.

"What impacted me was his commitment to
science itself. And that he wanted to teach me
the science he loved."

Ken admits, when he completed this science class he actually
didn't have a lot of self-esteem in the area of science. But, when
he got into the 6th grade science, "It was a breeze." By 7th grade
science he had a *love* for the subject.

He ended up going to college and studying biology, physics,
and chemistry. He knows this was a direct result of Mr. Ingle
who gave him such a love for science. Though he didn't know
it at the time, he was being trained to think in scientific
terms – and at a high level for his grade. From that point on,
he continued to be way ahead.

There was also another person who impacted Ken. He taught
him to really express himself creatively through art. As a result,
Ken ended up winning two art grants to go to college. That
teacher embraced Ken's love of his uncle's book drawing horses,
which guided him all the way up to sculpture and other artistic
endeavors. It helped him develop an eye for photography,
which he attributes to his love of art – an understanding of
composition and light.

The third person impacting Ken would be the person who got
him involved in being competitive in sports. He taught Ken a
lot about pushing himself physically… and also about balance.
He didn't do that so much intentionally just for Ken; he did it
with the mentorship of his entire team. It developed in Ken an
understanding that a person can be fantastic at all the things
he or she sets their mind to do.

"I told my mom when I was young, 'I don't think it's possible to be good at more than two things. If you're great at sports, you're not great at academics. If you're great at academics, you're not great at sports.'

"But I was wrong. There *is* a way to do it all. You have to have balance in your life to do it. And there's a constant struggle to maintain that balance. But I think that you can actually find out what's important to you and then make sure you have time for those things. If you do it right, you create excellence in all of them."

Academics, though, was not Ken's only area of early development. Though he was born in Rhode Island, within months after being born, he was whisked off to France for his dad's first military duty assignment. Ken would not return to the United States until age 12. At that point, he had been in 13 different places before the return.

For that reason, it was Ken's immediate family that impacted him most. His parents believed in character development. His mother was a full-time mom. And his dad was a military officer who taught his sons to be young officers in their bearing. "There's no doubt about it, we were a reflection on him and he made sure we knew that."

Both his parents especially stressed honesty. He would carry that character development into his college days... and beyond.

Ken's observations demonstrate the impact that experiences, in his case especially family experiences, can have on the development of a successful person. And, again, those experiences don't have to be linked to college, or any other type of formal education. They can come from personal study, or simply just observations one has in his or her daily routine.

All of these are linked, however, to a desire to learn.

Jim Vaughn is a lifelong student of human attitudes, habits, and skills that cause success in a person's life. Coupled with his observations of human behavior, he has over 50 years of experience in *intense* research. Both of these abilities have led him to the conclusion that anyone who has an inspiring goal, or wants to succeed at any level, *can* be successful.

Jim speaks of what he knows. He put together a very successful sales career applying the concepts of sales' masters such as Napoleon Hill in his book, *Think and Grow Rich*, and especially J. Douglas Edwards, in Jim's mind "the godfather of sales trainers." Edwards' "The Foundations of Modern Selling," now available as a digital recording series, was Jim's "go to" that he is convinced led to his success. As he modestly observes, "Edwards' recordings proved to be the single best investment I've ever made in my entire lifetime… because in my lifetime I have earned well over a million dollars."

Men like Hill and Edwards led to Jim's success, yes. But, there was also success because of his lifelong love of research.

That love, however, though linked to his beginnings, did not come from school. Jim admits he was a terrible student in school, always feeling like the dumbest kid in the classroom

– he stresses *always*. As he reflects on it, Jim never doubted he was the last student in the class to figure out what the teacher was talking about.

To be fair it wasn't necessarily because of Jim's lack of ability. In his elementary school, in the third grade, there was a serious teacher shortage. For all intents and purposes, he didn't really have a third-grade teacher. He actually had nine substitute teachers in nine months!

Worse, his class was in the school auditorium with three other classes going on all around his own class. So, there were four different teachers all teaching separate classes to a total of 120 students. Bedlam. And not an environment for learning.

> "As a result, I didn't get the third-grade material. I did not understand it at all. But they promoted me to the fourth grade anyway. And then it just continued: Year after year after year, I was just totally lost. You simply cannot build the fourth story of a building until you've completed the third.
>
> "And my third was never completed."

Jim was not deterred. Even though formal education was failing him, he *did* have a love for knowledge. He would pursue that desire… his own way.

He saw the only benefit that school had for him personally was it prepared him to be a lifelong learner, a lifetime researcher. And for that he is eternally grateful.

Once he identified his love of pursuing truth, Jim personally, and privately, became an excellent student. He reflects, then he became very, *very* hungry for knowledge, and gaining understanding into the things that really interested him. For that reason, he began to study harder than most anybody else he knew.

Jim is a strong advocate that a person needs to learn what they need to learn. In his case, this caused him to become his own best teacher. He firmly believes that is the best thing you could ever do for yourself.

> "Now, why is this important? Because schools typically shortchange students by not teaching them the skills that pay the bills. The one-size-fits-all style of teaching methods hasn't changed in what, the last 1,500 years? Not everybody learns best in that environment. Again, I was a perfect example.
>
> "To me, classrooms have become learning factories whose goal it is to produce identical thinkers and doers. That process kills individuality and personal creativity."

At an early age, ahead of his peers, Jim came to understand a truth that even some adults never learn in their entire lifetime. Because, within his circle of friends and acquaintances, he didn't know anybody that was as interested in the things that *he* was interested in. It made him kind of a loner.

Yet, even as a kid, that never bothered him – "It just didn't." To this day it doesn't bother him when people don't think like he does.

> "And that's fine. I give everybody their freedom to think what they want to think, do what they want to do. But, they have to be willing to accept the outcome of their thoughts, feelings, and actions.
>
> "Whether positive choices or negative choices, there are *always* consequences from what we think, say, or do."

Sometimes our actions, and their consequences, are not based so much on available information as from that of a hunch. Acting on one's instincts also produces results. Jim relates one of those instances. He acted on a hunch as he passed a bookstore…

In 1961, at a rather young age, he came across the book *Think and Grow Rich* by Napoleon Hill. That one book changed his life forever. It gave him a level of self-confidence that he had never known before. And it gave him an understanding that he didn't need to follow the path that everybody else was following.

The one standout principle that Jim got from Hill's book was that successful people always deliver more than what people expect of them. As a result of that insight, he developed a legendary relationship with his customers because there was nobody among his competitors who would provide more for them than he did.

He cites as an example: If a problem arose, the customer saw that Jim would go out of his way to resolve it. And he wouldn't quit until it *was* resolved!

Reading Hill on his own, even at an early age, also caused Jim to realize that his success was not dependent on what he had learned in the classroom. There were principles of success that could be gained from personal seeking. That began his lifetime search for other teachers, successful like Napoleon Hill, who understood and taught the principles of success.

And that is why Jim muses that one of the biggest surprises for him in life is why everyone doesn't take the time to learn these same principles of success! Didn't they realize that the biggest advantage to learning these things is that when other people don't think it's important to do so, it means there are fewer people to compete with you as you pursue your dreams? It just makes sense to him that pursuing this knowledge works to your own advantage.

He is firmly convinced that 19 out of 20 people just don't want to put in the effort. They're floating through life adrift, and as long as they earn enough money to buy groceries and keep a roof over their head, that's all they think life is about. He feels this is unfortunate because, if a person is willing to put in the effort, life will give him or her more than that.

What many people fail to realize, he reflects, is the wealth of information, *career-building* information, that is available today. He is amazed they only use their electronic devices for amusement rather than advancement. "I guess they don't have the same thirst for knowledge that I do." He reflects, *sadly* so.

Continuing with one of the themes Jim Vaughn raises, there are always consequences for the decisions we make in life. And, often, those consequences impact not just ourselves, but others as well. We must be constantly mindful of that. Ken MacArthur learned that lesson in his own origins.

Ken McArthur, best-selling author of *Impact: How to Get Noticed, Motivate Millions and Make a Difference in a Noisy World*, has enabled thousands of people to achieve amazing impact by championing the philosophy that partnerships and collaboration build value for everyone.

The popular host of jvAlert Live – a series of live events that bring top-level marketers together to create multi-million-dollar joint venture relationships – he creates incredible, intense impact for product launches and multi-million-dollar profits in surprisingly short timeframes.

Ken McArthur is also the creator of AffiliateShowcase.com, a pioneering affiliate program search engine and directory system, and the founder of the MBS Internet Research Center, which conducted the world's largest survey ever attempted on the subject of creating and launching successful information products.

Selected by Fast Company as one of the 20 Most Influential People Online, Ken's powerful call to action, "The Impact Manifesto: You Make A Difference Whether You Want To Or Not" was selected for publication by Seth Godin's brainchild "Change This."

"The Impact Manifesto" is currently being produced as a short film that will benefit over 100 non-profit organizations by raising funds and awareness for their programs.

Ken is also the producer of a new feature film, "The Impact Factor Movie" which challenges us to realize we *all* have an impact – whether we want to or not – on thousands of people who we touch in our day-to-day lives by demonstrating that simple things make a *huge* difference.

Ken McArthur's Impact Action Team took a small group of people working together and managed to get a simple message of hope out to over 19.1 *million* people in less than 30 days to help prevent teen suicide!

The insights that would lead to these successes are rooted in Ken's origins. Though he admits he doesn't actually remember a lot about his elementary school years, he does remember that in the early days he went to school the first time in Miami, Florida. But he has just a glimpse of it in his recollection: A vague picture of being at a school and a crossing guard being there. Academically though, and unlike most, he doesn't remember a thing beyond that.

It was then he moved to Colorado halfway through his second-grade year. There, he feels he was a pretty ordinary kid that was growing up in the Four Corners area of Colorado.

His father was a Presbyterian minister who used to travel the Four Corners region where Arizona, New Mexico, Utah, and Colorado all come together. As a pastor, his dad would travel 200 miles on a Sunday preaching in the oil fields of Utah, in the mountains of Colorado, and in the bean fields of the Four Corners areas. That ministry led him to see all kinds of different people.

Ken and his family used to go along and were the church choir. So, his father's ministry got Ken to start singing at an early age. He reflects that it was not necessarily the macho thing to do. But it turned out to work for him because in high school he didn't have any athletic advantages.

Regarding athleticism, he notes that he was third string out of three strings on the football team for a little bit in his junior year. Notwithstanding, he can say he was undefeated in wrestling. Though the truth was, he had two draws and beat only one person. His only claim to athletic prowess.

It was singing in the choir with his family where Ken's musical ability paid off. Using that as a springboard, he tried out for the school musical when he was a freshman in high school. He admits he was a dork, but his musical ability got him cast in the leading role... playing opposite the most gorgeous senior girl in the school!

"If you are a high school kid right now, I want you to think about that!

"I was living off my stardom when, all of a sudden, my dad was transferred to a different job that was farther up the western slope of Colorado. That meant I had to transfer to *another* school.

"If anyone had been through that kind of experience of having to change from one school to another, they know it can be plenty tough. I was lucky because, being the son of a preacher, I came in contact with some of the kids from school at church. This meant I got to pair up with some of the older boys, which

> proved helpful in fitting in. I again eventually became involved in choir and in band and in drama. At the new school I also became involved in the school plays."

It was during this period that he also started plinking away at a guitar, eventually becoming pretty good at it. He even started writing his own songs. He also learned a life-lesson in that if he wrote mistakes in those songs people wouldn't realize it because they didn't know the way the song was supposed to be!

During get-togethers where he sat around living rooms with small crowds of kids, he would sing his songs; sometimes sad songs, the kind of songs that only teenagers can write. And he saw the emotional impact such songs had.

It was in high school Ken met the guy who had a great impact on him. He was the football hero, was valedictorian of the class, and was a student body president. He was the guy who already had been accepted to the Air Force Academy. Everybody just knew he was going to be a superstar in whatever he undertook.

Ken clearly remembers this young man coming to one of the living room events. It was there that Ken was playing his guitar and singing his own songs that he had written. The football hero listened to Ken's playing and, later they both went out on the porch to talk.

> "He told me my songs had changed his life. I thought about that, honestly, and was a bit skeptical. I didn't really think for a moment that I changed his life. But, what if I did? Here was a person who was going to the Air

Force Academy. One day he might be leading troops on some far-away battlefield.

"Maybe, just maybe, some little thing that I sang which brought some emotion out in him could impact the future of hundreds of people. And many more over the course of his lifetime."

It was then, in high school, Ken discovered the true meaning of impact; the fact that we all make a difference. Whether its intentional or not, even tiny little things can have an impact that will ripple down through the years from person to person. One person impacting another. One person definitely impacting thousands of people over an entire lifetime.

Ken often considers this insight gained so early in his life: What could be accomplished if people proactively used the arts, the sciences, the technology that they have, and intentionally went out to make a positive difference.

This understanding was reinforced, he feels, as a result of the impact his parents had on his life. He realized he was lucky enough to have parents who truly encouraged him. They taught him that he could do anything that he set his mind to. Ken views this as a huge gift that he had early on in his life.

Through high school Ken was mostly a B student, with some A's in math classes. He knew the secret of straight A's was hard work. But, he admits, he wasn't attracted to very many books. So, he wasn't a straight A student. He was, however, president of thespians and president of the National Honor Society. There *was* accomplishment in high school!

Once he graduated, he moved on to college, where, he admits, he was a little bit lost. Yes, he was in college, but he didn't know exactly what he wanted to do with that education. Ken reflects this is not unusual for a college freshman. Nor, for that matter, for some college seniors!

> "Just keep that in mind when sometimes it feels like there are no opportunities, there are no options, that nothing will ever work out. That's the time to have faith and you need to realize that the world's here with opportunities that go beyond what you might this very minute be seeing.

> "A healthy perspective takes a look at the boundless and endless opportunities you might have before you. A part of that perspective is to realize that if one way is blocked, often another opens up. In time there are so many other ways, other options, if you just look for them."

For those who attend, and eventually complete, college, it should provide an origin, a beginning, to a career. But often there are other influences. At the time Ken was growing up, it was during the build-up of the Vietnam War. That *had* to be considered in any choice he made. As one can see, we're influenced by not only our academics.

As a result of these experiences early in his life, his origins, Ken firmly believes everyone is here on the planet for a purpose.

He sees that we all have our own unique pathways – the things that makes each of us great as an individual. It is that uniqueness, shared with others, which, for him, is the way that we can work together to make things so much better.

> "I also think that we all may not have discovered 'a' purpose yet. Frankly, we actually have many purposes. And it's always the smallest things that we do in life that have the biggest impact. So, I think there's lots of purpose in life. If we know the direction that we're headed in and if we have the common sense to use all of the different resources and people and relationships that we have, we can have a bigger impact."

Ken's insight, as with the other successful people in this chapter, comes from a lifetime of experience. And that experience had a foundation… their beginnings. Having looked at some of the issues that are related to origins, the question is, What are *your* origins telling you?

This is an important reflection. A solid consideration on where you have come from, is a key to understanding where you might ultimately be called to go.

And nothing confirms that direction more than that almost-quiet, barely-tangible, yet always-distinct, "voice" found deep within us. That longing-influence which urges us to go in our own distinctly unique direction in life. This effect is often referred to as our Calling.

2   CALLING

Your profession is not what brings home your weekly paycheck,
your profession is what you're put here on earth to do,
with such passion and such intensity that
it becomes spiritual in calling.

Vincent van Gogh

call-ing n. a strong inner attraction or appeal
to a particular activity: MISSION.

The consistent testimony of men and women who have gone on to success is that at some point in time they felt this deep inner desire to accomplish. This desire became such a driving force that, against all odds and opposition, they felt they must go forward. The consistent word used to describe that deep inner desire was *irresistible.*

Some felt this calling early in life, in their youth. Some later, even as a *senior* citizen. Equally as consistent was the desire to not only be successful, but to produce something of value that could be used now and for future generations. The calling, then, was not self-centered, even if the desire for success could be called so.

It is interesting to note that this deep inner desire, this calling, also provided the future successful person with an understanding of their purpose in life. Again, that purpose served the greater good of all, not just the person feeling the call.

Ironically, sometimes the call was a definite challenge in that to accomplish the future goal, the immediate skill-set was, at the time of the calling, completely inadequate! But, whether prepared or unprepared, each individual found an equally deep and abiding joy when he or she reflected on undertaking the task.

It is worth noting that this joy is the signpost that *this* mission, this goal, is for you.

Jessica Peterson is the Founder of the Simply WOW Agency and Customer WOW Project. WOW is about people and relationships which bring richness across a person's life, as well as their client's lives—richness in spirit and in celebrating success, as well as in financial security. Jessica's background is a 20-year career in banking, mortgage, finance, and insurance. She has always been one of the top performers, winning numerous top sales and employee awards, while creating and implementing strategies utilizing social media.

Jessica has written five books currently available. She was awarded the 2015 Top 100 Women In The World award. She was also awarded the 2015 Top 12 Spirited Women Award. In 2015, she was honored to actually deliver a Technology, Entertainment, and Design (TED) speech in Colorado.

Jessica has developed a proprietary 4-step plan of action to help her clients grow their business in social media. Using her 4-step success plan, she has grown an affiliate team to over 3,000 sales associates worldwide in just one year. That is one of the reasons why she has been selected as a top speaker and trainer out of 260,000 people.

Jessica had the good fortune to know at an early age that she had the spirit of an entrepreneur.

She remembers when she was 10 years old and her father told her if she wanted fancier clothes, if she wanted some food outside of home, that she was going to have to work for it. So, from age 10 to 18, she went to work for three doctors cleaning their medical offices every week. Jessica even then was beginning to realize the concept of running her own operation.

There is another curious aspect regarding her being an entrepreneur. When she was a kid, she had Barbie dolls like her friends. But, all *her* Barbies were single! And they were all independent women. Jessica would map out their jobs, even their entire careers. This included where they worked and when they got raises and how much they volunteered in the community!

> "So when I used to go to my friend's house and they would want to play Barbies, for them it was always Barbie is married and a housewife. I thought, Why? Does Barbie not want to volunteer? Why does Barbie not have goals or a desire to be independent? Or strive to be better? Nothing against my friends,

I just came to realize we all have different dreams."

Then there is Lane Ethridge's experience. He is currently known as the world's fastest Lane Changer. The founder of Changing Lanes International, a 4-time National Bestselling author including his most recent *Life in the Fast Lane*, a transformational speaker, professional sales trainer, and innovative entrepreneur, Lane helps committed entrepreneurs accelerate their success.

A former public school math teacher, Lane's heart is focused on teaching and educating. As an entrepreneur, he has been able to create six figures in three industries because he is one of the best networkers, leveraging his proficient communication skills. Abundant in his approach to collaborative advancements, Lane excels as a premier coaching leader, personal coach, and mentor for his clients.

He is a phenomenal visionary as a creative marketing and speaker trainer. He founded Changing Lanes International, a business around empowering entrepreneurs to maximize their gifts and skills to drive their business forward. After seeing many take the low road on the path to creating success, he found his passion for helping others determine the right lane for them in order to remain on the high road to greatness.

Moreover, he has an uncanny ability to capture his clients' gifts and talents as well as their story to craft their message to share with the world. Most importantly, Lane has the unparalleled ability to take a client's story and help him or her turn it into a signature keynote and monetize it effectively. He then teaches them the skills to empower others and leverage their uniqueness so that they can maximize their value in the marketplace, captivating new prospects and acquiring new clients of their own. He is known for turning a person from merely being an author into a renowned authority!

In contrast to Jessica Peterson, Lane Etheridge is, like many successful entrepreneurs, one who got the call as a *second* vocation. This makes him, as he describes himself, "a lane changer."

He graduated college at the age of 23 and immediately started to work in the middle school system in Maryland, as a pre-algebra teacher. About two years later he decided to make "a career shift." As a result of that decision, he relocated to San Diego.

This career "lane change," was all the result of reading a book called, *Rich Dad, Poor Dad*. He notes that a lot of entrepreneurs read it. At that time in his life, the concepts were so revolutionary to him. That's because his world view, his education, and his personal growth were not anywhere near where they are now. But, back then, he knew he was being called to something else. He quit teaching to became an entrepreneur.

To be fair, in part his decision was based on what he saw as a teacher. In a short period of time that he taught, he came to disbelieve in the systems that were in place by the educational administration for which he worked. Too many things he saw were contradictory. They especially didn't want a teacher to be creative. It was then he began to find it difficult to teach 12-, 13-, and 14-year olds to follow what he no longer believed in.

"Don't misunderstand, I loved the idea of shaping the minds of our teenagers, because I identified with them. I was a young teacher, at the time. I fell in love with the idea of tutoring; mentoring right within the school system. Of shaping and helping them. Not just with Algebra, but with character development. It was my first real admiration with the concept of supporting, of helping other people and mentoring in some capacity. But the school system itself was confining.

"*Rich Dad, Poor Dad* was really my first exposure to the opportunity that there was a different route you could take. The honest truth is a lot of people will quit there. That's what most want-to-preneurs do. They say, 'Okay great, I have an idea – I want to do something different,' and they get stuck in not going forward. Sadly, ten years later they are doing the same exact thing they had wanted to get away from a decade earlier.

"So, I took action. And began a new, *second* career."

Then there is Coach Andre M. "A.M." Williams. He specializes in helping coaches and consultants use and leverage communication to increase their sales. This includes mastering the art of achieving more by utilizing existing talents and resources, as well as communicating value to win in business and to win in life. He trains in the art of value-based selling.

His intent is to grow his client's business and to assist them to achieve more freedom in regards to their time.

One of Coach A.M. Williams' programs is "Leverage Without Limits." Employing his philosophy there, he has inspired and empowered professional coaches, consultants, network marketers, professors, and even corporate managers to become better leaders as they increase their sales and their efficiency by as much as 50%. In this way they are able to enjoy more time freedom and lifestyle freedom as they increase their financial freedom.

Unlike most, Coach A.M. realized the call to be an entrepreneur was one of expediency.

He didn't actually choose to be an entrepreneur because he felt led to start his own business. Life's circumstances dictated that decision for him.

It happened when he got the diagnosis about his incomplete paraplegia. Because of that illness, he could no longer perform his then job duties. He was literally forced to find a way to make sure that he could pay his bills and maintain some quality of life.

It was then he decided to leave a very well-paying job with a financial institution and start a business. From his options, he chose to do insurance and investments, a business, he reflects, that left little room for failure.

With this task in mind, he went out and took his insurance test, which he passed on the first try. Then he had to go out and do recruiting. The requirement was to bring in at least three clients. Coach A.M. admits he knocked that out pretty fast. By the time he got certified he had already qualified three levels up. It was all very rewarding for a man around 28 years of age starting a new career.

> "Interesting enough, there was no specific event that the doctors could tie my illness in to. They said that they didn't actually know how it got there. This was really more frustrating, because if it couldn't be attributed to something, it made it harder to understand. When it just comes out-of-the-blue, it's even more trying.

> "I initially went to the doctor to see if I had pulled a muscle from lifting weights. But at the examination they told me I had to be admitted to the hospital for surgery. Life was changing for me very quickly."

Coach A.M. was immediately admitted into the hospital to have that surgery. He walked into the hospital and several hours later, when they asked him to move his feet, he couldn't do it. His whole life changed *very* quickly. He had absolutely no preparation... and had to adapt really quickly.

> "So, I think that had a lot to do with my ability to function as a business operator – what I now consider a business steward – and start up my own company. I didn't have any options. My back was against the wall."

Though Coach A.M.'s situation is not the usual way one is called to a profession or undertaking, it is a reality that some must also face. It is important to realize that even with adversity, success is possible.

Ken MacArthur, the producer of the feature film, "The Impact Factor Movie," whom we met in chapter 1, was like Jessica Peterson; he received the call early in life. The difference was that he acted on that call just as early. And it led to more callings!

Even though his dad was a minister, his father always had a vision of someday starting his own business. That entrepreneurial spirit was passed down to Ken. He started a bicycle shop as a boy in a beat-down shed. That spunk and vision has kept going his entire life.

From the bicycle shop Ken branched out and started mowing lawns with an old electric lawn mower. He built up enough business that with the money mowing lawns he could buy a gas-powered lawn mower. For him, that was a big deal.

He also ran a fish store when he was age 21. What made that so exciting for him was this business actually went on to set the course of his life. At that early age he realized he didn't have a boss telling him what to do, or how to do it. That sense of freedom was something he wanted to experience his entire working days.

As a result of this freedom, Ken took a rundown, old, mostly tropical fish store, and fixed it up. He tore out the entire insides and made it a better place. This added to his sense that he was adding value to the world. As the store succeeded, he eventually carried all kinds of pets.

He then began a recording studio. Because of his interest in music, he wanted to become involved in the recording field. So he could do his *own* music.

Ken took the risk and went out with a credit card and bought a four-track recorder at a high-end stereo store. While there, he just happened to notice that the store had a beat-up old building that was nearby. It had been an old pool hall that was no longer in use. It was totally dilapidated.

Ken offered the owners that if he came in and fixed this building up and turned it into a recording studio, would they give him the first six months rent-free. They agreed, and so he immediately started working on the interior.

He now had a building to work from, and a recorder to work with, but he didn't have any microphones or other needed equipment. So, he went around to the bands in the area and offered them free time in his full-fledged recording studio for their microphone or a speaker or whatever other piece of equipment that he needed.

> "It was an adventure. Yes, I did it partly out of necessity – partly out of an arrogance – but I was working to fix something up. My business location and needed equipment came first. But, in giving those bands a recording studio to get that equipment, it helped fix the bands up too."

As you can see, Ken took each calling and turned it into success. The moral: A person need not be limited to one calling.

Eric Lofholm is a naturally gifted teacher who has become an internationally recognized master sales trainer. For the past 18 years, he has been sharing his ideas for increasing sales and profits worldwide. He offers expert training for both corporate sales departments and for individuals who want to improve their sales skills. As a result, he has helped over 10,000 students increase their sales income. This has helped generate nearly $500-million in revenue in the last two decades.

Eric honed his skills as a trainer working with Tony Robbins, the renowned entrepreneur, author, and life coach, from 1997 to 1999, before actually starting his own company, Eric Lofholm International. His methods are now used in over 500 different companies including Aflac, Century 21, Prudential, Morgan Stanley, World Financial Group, and a host of others. He is also the author of 10 different best-selling books on Amazon.

Eric's call to business was also early in life. And though we shall see in subsequent chapters a formal education can be helpful at times towards gaining success, Eric shows it is not always necessary.

> "I had collected sports cards like many kids do. So, I ran a baseball card business my junior year of high school.

> "In 1987, there was a series of rookies and the rookie cards that were of high value; cards like Mark McGwire, Barry Bonds, Will Clark, and a few others. They were all rookies that year. I figured out that if I bought a box of cards, I would get a number of these

rookies mixed in. A box, then, was worth more opened than unopened.

"With that in mind, I went and was able to arrange a $4,000 loan from one of my family members. I went out and purchased several hundred thousand cards with this money and started my own baseball card business.

"I did about $20,000 in revenue that summer! This was the first entrepreneurial thing that I did and it laid the groundwork for what I'm doing today.

"After I graduated high school, however, I first went to a local community college. I spent five years there and never actually graduated; never got a 2-year Associate in Arts degree.

"My calling, I came to find out, was in hands-on business… not academics!"

As can be seen here, the calling, that inward desire to accomplish something, is what "gets the ball rolling." And it is unique to each person. When, where, how, and why it starts will be tailored to every individual.

Notwithstanding, whether one feels the call early in life, or late; whether one decides to move forward out of choice, or circumstances; whether one is college educated or not, each person will encounter a decision-point. The consistent description for this point is most often called the *Crossroad*.

3   CROSSROADS

There are crossroads in life where choosing
the direction to pursue is critical.

Steven Redhead

Cross-road *n*. a crucial point at which a
decision must be made: TIME TO CHOOSE.

Throughout life, we reach many points where important decisions must be made. Very often we don't realize these are critical decision points until later when we reflect back on them. This holds true for people who have gone on to achieve success.

But, whether we realize them at the time, or later in reflection, crossroads will be consistently faced on your own path to success. It is the wise person who realizes this early and so is not blindsided when those crossroads are met.

Yet, many a successful person will tell you there is at least one time in their life where events themselves stepped in to make a difference. It has often been referred to as the "Divine Intervention Moment."

Dr. Will Moreland is an internationally respected global thought leader and strategist, who has traveled the world training leaders at every organizational level. He has a doctorate in Strategic Leadership Development from Minnesota Graduate School. Dr. Will has worked with such significant companies as American Airlines, Boeing, Edward Jones, and Intel.

One quickly sees he is very much an expert in leadership development, company culture development, team building, and diversity and inclusion implementation. He has developed a leadership training program and philosophy where he teaches employees how to become leaders where they are. As a business strategist Dr. Will has grown several of his brands to million-dollar levels as well as helped others build, brand, and expand their own businesses.

It should also be noted, he is a bestselling author of over 40 books covering the topics of leadership, motivation, and productivity. Further, he has served in the United States Army, being twice deployed to the conflict in the Balkans as part of the American military response to that region in the 1990s. He received an Honorable Discharge at the end of his enlistment.

> "One day I'm walking in the mall and a gentleman by the name of Corey Oliver comes up to me. Corey is an Army recruiter. He looks me directly in the eye and asked, 'Excuse me, have you ever thought about going into the Army?'
>
> "To be honest, I have to admit that when I woke up that day, I had not thought about it!

But in that moment, in that very second, I looked at Corey and said, 'Come on – let's go. I'm ready.' He looked at me a little startled. 'What?' I said, 'Come on – let's go. I'm ready. I'll sign up right now.' Before the sun went down that day, I signed up to go into the Army. So, that's how I got into military.

"I had never thought about the military before. It had never been a part of 'my plan.' But looking at it now, it was one of the best decisions of my life."

As you can see, sometimes the crossroad drops in out of nowhere. Yet, there are other times when you can clearly see it coming.

Chris Salem is an accomplished international keynote speaker, change strategist, corporate sales mindset trainer, best-selling author, radio host, and wellness advocate partnering with entrepreneurs, business leaders, and corporate sales professionals to have sustainable success at the next level by resolving the root cause to their mindset barriers. He has a special passion for empowering them to take their business and life to another level by operating in the solution rather than the problem.

Chris shares from experience what has worked successfully for him through understanding the root cause behind the effects of limiting patterns in one's business or personal life. He is the originator of the term *Prosperneur*™ — an individual whose health and wealth are in alignment in a way that leads to true prosperity. His book *Master Your Inner Critic: Resolve the Root*

Cause – Create Prosperity addresses this and went international best seller in November 2016.

In his high school years, Chris was a baseball player and, at the time, this was back during the 80's, he had long hair. He admits it wasn't down to his waist, but it was long for a guy even in those days.

The coach he was playing for was very conservative and traditional. Chris knew there would be a problem. And to this day, he still thinks that was the reason he did not make the team. He is sure it was not as a result of his playing ability, which was more than adequate to be chosen. It was the coach's perception of how Chris looked based upon his hair length.

This made Chris feel he was trying to tell Chris who he *should* be. That seemed wrong to Chris, so he stood his ground and didn't cut his hair in order to make the team. He realized as he did it, that he was at a decision-point.

> "I did not, however, allow that experience, which was very painful in the beginning, to hold me back. I was able to revamp and find another way to play in another league outside of high school. There, I demonstrated skills that provided the opportunity to be considered at some colleges for my ability.
>
> "You can't allow somebody to dictate your talents and abilities. Only you can do that. You should choose to accept your God-given gifts and to capitalize and enhance your strengths, rather than your weaknesses.

"So, I made a decision that the only judge was my Higher Power and myself. I can either go and overcome the criticism, or I could have crawled into a hole.

"That experience of being rejected by the high school coach, while it could have worked against me causing a negative impact upon my life, actually reinforced my belief in standing my ground. I *knew* I needed to be who I was, not someone that somebody else thought I should be. I also came to realize you are not going to be able to please everyone."

As you can see, decision points, those crossroads we each must face, are usually a place for a life's learning lesson.

Jessica Peterson, whom we met in chapter 2 liking her Barbie to be an independent businesswoman, confirms this. As we saw, she had an entrepreneurial spirit at a young age. But she really didn't act on it until around age 23. It was about then that she had that *ah-ha* moment.

"I was working a job, sitting there working really hard. I am not saying there is anything wrong with that. But working so hard and pushing myself so much for so little pay. I just had this feeling I wanted to create my own destiny. I wanted to write my own story. I felt as if life was limiting me as I worked for a corporation.

"I recall the bank I worked for. It was a 32-hour-a-week position that seemed to need twice that number of hours to accomplish the tasks! I worked really hard: Anybody who knows me knows I'm all about let's create systems, success, time management – let's move and shake and get things done. So, when I say I needed help, I really needed help.

"I recall saying, 'I really need help. I really need help,' and they never listened. When I finally left, I discovered they had to hire two 40-hour people to replace me.

"It had definitely been time for me to move on!"

Paul Hoyt is the owner and principal consultant with Paul Hoyt Management Group. He's a best-selling author with over 40-years of experience in leading teams to improve profitability and productivity. He's an expert in helping new and growing businesses develop their strategic plans, create financial models, write business plans, and fund and execute their growth strategies. He has enjoyed tremendous success in helping businesses, of all sizes, achieve their goals and exit strategy objectives.

Paul is the creator of the Awakened CEO System – a powerful collection of tools and programs to help CEOs and entrepreneurs grow their businesses and gain wisdom in the process.

Paul also created the highly-acclaimed, online training programs, "The Business Survival Boot Camp" and the "Awakened CEO Foundations Program," giving small business owners the guidance they need to make great decisions and implement a winning company culture from the start.

He is the author of two different business books, *The Foundation Factor* (which he wrote in 2004) and *The Capitol Coaching Program* (which he wrote in 2010) which helps entrepreneurs learn the fundamentals of raising capital.

In addition, Paul is also the best-selling author of *The Practice of Awakening to the First Light of Joy* in 2013 – a collection of poems, meditations and insights for personal and spiritual growth; and two previous inspirational works *Remember a Simple, Gentle and Powerful Pathway to Your Management Way, to Your Management Potential* in 2005, an inspirational CD, and *The Practice of Awakening* in 2010.

For most successful persons, there is not just one decision point, but many. Paul reflects on his three different landmark moments.

The first one was when he was in high school, Geometry class. He reflects he was doing his usual thing, not really listening to the lectures because he'd worked ahead in the book and was busy causing trouble in the classroom.

His teacher called him up after the class and told Paul he thought Paul was bored. Paul was honest with him and admitted he *was* bored. He let the teacher know he was "kind of a couple chapters ahead." It was then the teacher challenged Paul… to finish the textbook as quickly as he could. The teacher offered that if Paul did, the teacher would move on with him and let Paul study some other subjects in Math.

This challenge excited Paul. Who would have thought?...

"I quickly got through the Geometry book over the next 30 days and the teacher began to give me other assignments. From other books he provided, I studied Metric Algebra and then Calculus. This teacher was somebody who really believed in me. Instead of telling me to be quiet and get control of myself, he challenged me to learn.

"That milestone of having a teacher, one who not only saw that I was bright, but who also challenged me, really, *really* impacted me. And the challenges were not just superficial. That teacher was giving me much more difficult mathematics than was required by the class. It provided me with the belief for the next steps in my life's journey. I really believed, at that point, that I was a very, very bright person capable of greatness. It was because somebody believed in me, challenged me, and mentored me towards the direction to excel."

Paul's second milestone happened in college. He awoke up one day and realized that he was not happy, that he was actually a miserable guy. He looked around at his then current circumstances and realized how stressed out he was; how anxious, bordering on bitterness. That bitterness demonstrated itself through sarcasm, and a cynical attitude. He noted he had very few friends.

> "At that moment, a decision point, I decided I was going to change that. I decided that I was going to dedicate a large portion of my life towards being as happy as I could completely be and, coupled with that, being the best person that I could be.

> "Since that decision, about 45 years ago, I've been working on myself every day. That milestone was a profound sense of self-awareness. In reflection I see it as an act of courage to admit to myself that I was not as happy, even though I had a lot of talents and abilities. They weren't enough. Even with them, I was just not happy."

The third real milestone crossroad actually caused him to break from the corporate world and to go into his own business in 2001. At the time, he was running a 20-million-dollar business unit for a very large telecommunications company. But the business itself was not doing well. This caused the company to have to reorganize. Unfortunately for Paul, this reorganized him right out of his position.

To add insult to injury, two months before they gave him his walking papers, he had won a prize for being one of the top five employees at the company. They gave him a $20,000 bonus, which was a huge amount of money back in 2001. He was on top of the world, believing how great he was. He still ponders on that old saying, "Pride comes before a fall."

The next thing he knew, he found himself out on the street. Not only was he unemployed, but for those who can remember, the U.S. was in the midst of a big recession in 2001 caused, in large measure, by the events of September 11th. On top of all that, his second son was just starting college. Not just any college, but Stanford University with a tuition back in those days of about $40,000 per year.

At this crossroad, where he did not have any income anymore and there were no jobs to be found, Paul looked around and made a decision. The answer came to him in less than 10 seconds: He was going to start his own business. And this time, now with 18 years corporate experience, he knew he was better prepared to do just that. At the age of 50-years old, he decided to create the Hoyt Management Group and began to work as a small business consultant.

> "I'm sure I was a little anxious; a bit nervous. But there was no real hesitation or resistance, nothing that ever caused me to question my own ability to do it... and do it extremely well. If anything, I was probably a little overconfident about my ability. Which by the way, as most know, is really insecurity; insecurity and arrogance are two sides of the same coin.

> "As with most people, that insecurity was because I was still working on myself, progressing through my own personal development. The truth is, that development never stops, regardless of your age.

"In any case, I felt like if anybody was prepared, I was prepared, and I was eager for the opportunity – I was ready to go. Here it is 35 years later after making that decision to go into business for myself and I'm *still* working on myself… every single day."

For those, like these successful business people here, who can identify immediately that they are at a crossroads, a life's major decision point, that insight can produce a calmness that the person who is blindsided cannot usually feel. It is helpful, therefore, to quickly identify that you are at a crossroad point in order to make the wisest decision possible.

Once that decision is made and a direction set, the next order of business is to develop a plan. Without it, success most often is fleeting… if ever attained at all.

4   PLANNING

Planning is bringing the future into the present
so that you can do something about it now.

Alan Lakein

Plan-ning n. the act or process of establishing
future goals: PREPARATION.

Planning, as Alan Lakein has noted above, is the process of going from your desire of being successful to actually achieving that success. It is charting out the process by which that success will be attained.

There is a procedure to the planning process. First, you have to determine what your actual goal(s) is. Be specific. As an example, if you want to start a business, state exactly what that business is. This is your vision for the future, to create that company. It is your aiming point. Another example one could use is the goal of wanting to go to college. Specifically identify which one. It is a good idea to actually write down your goal. This is usually referred to as a *vision statement.*

Next, continuing with the new business example, specify exactly what good or service will be provided. This is your mission, how you will make this business customer-friendly, i.e. *needed*. For the college-bound hopeful, the mission would be to get good grades. This would make him or her more appealing to the college of their choice, i.e. the college would *want* them! Write down a simple, compelling statement of how you will make yourself needed or wanted. This is referred to as a *mission statement*.

The third step is, for many, the hardest. At this point you must take a hard look at where you are currently at. Here is the hard part: Be honest. This is not time for wishful thinking. The hard facts must be faced.

As an example, if the business requires $10,000 to get it up and running and you are currently penny-less, no amount of wishful thinking will overcome your financial bind. So, you have to be "brutally" truthful with yourself. Similarly, the college-hopeful must take a hard look at his or her current grades in deciding to which college he or she will apply.

The difference between where you currently are and where you eventually hope to be is often referred to as the "delta." Delta is the Greek letter for "d," which becomes a shorthand for the word "difference."

It is at this point that you begin to list what needs to be done to overcome any "difference." This analysis will produce what is individually called the Key Results Area (KRA). There will probably be many of them!

For our example of the business-hopeful, the KRA here would be to raise the money for the new business. By making a list of relatives, friends, and known philanthropists, action is taken that will identify individuals who might lend money to bridge that $10,000 "delta" gap and fulfill that KRA. For the college-hopeful, the KRA might be the need to get better grades. An acceptable action to fulfill it would be the decision to buckle-down in his or her studies.

As noted, one vision through its stated mission can produce any number of KRAs. You are not, as in our examples, in all likelihood only going to have one. But, by establishing Key Result Areas, you can literally chart your success in attaining your goal(s).

You should be mindful you need to be flexible. KRAs can change as results occur. Be willing and open to change when and where necessary. However, don't get sidetracked. If you find you are changing your KRAs often, usually on a whim, there is a problem. The word "key" should be your guide. It means "important." If the new area is a petty – or "pet" – project, it is not "key." Act accordingly.

Jim Vaughn (Chapter 1), whom we saw had committed himself to being a life-long learner, has used that learning to sculpture a near-perfect planning process for success.

He advises: Step One, you must figure out *what* you want. (Wasn't it the famous New York Yankee, Yogi Berra, who said, "If you don't know where you're going, you'll never get there!"?)

Step Two is to figure out *why* you want it. Your motivation speaks a lot about who you are, your character.

The Third Step is *how* to get it going. Jim thinks this third step is the easiest part of all. Because he thinks it's harder to figure out the *what* you want.

From his perspective on this 3-step process, Jim has observed over the years that people are always saying they want this or that. But they don't do anything about it. That tells him they really don't *want* it. They just want to talk about it. As far as he is concerned, real desire, authentic motivation, always produces action.

And, for him, that motivation to be a super successful person is not external. Like *only* going to seminars. The super achiever is constantly seeking knowledge on their own, like reading "a ton of books." Thus, he sees motivation as internal. Because they have identified *what* they want, they're not willing to settle for less.

It is at that point Jim's view is just like Stephanie Frank's: All of a person's dreams, desires, ambitions – their goals – are all possible as long as they stay focused and committed to their *why*. This focus leads naturally to clearly defining action and activity, i.e., making plans that will be executed daily over time.

> "One last thought about acting on your plan:
> As you work this process, the trick is to ignore
> how you feel and do it anyway. I say again,
> whatever you have to do, ignore how you feel.
> I don't care how you feel – do it *anyway*…
> especially if you don't *feel* like doing it!"

It is also important to remember that planning should not just be on "the immediate." People who are real leaders are always looking to the future. They are visionary… and plan accordingly. Actions have consequences, a ripple effect. Like a chess game, it is important to see many "moves ahead." Jim stresses this.

He also feels every person has a responsibility to the "future-you." This is because every day of a person's life there's two of themselves that they are looking after. You're looking after the person you are today, but you also need to be looking out after the person you will become.

From those who have gone on before him, Jim *knows* a day is going to come when a person will be in their sixties, seventies, eighties, and they might have run up a lot of medical bills. If that person has not prepared for that, begging for service might turn out to be their only option. To avoid such future complications, long-term planning is a must for Jim.

As a result of his own long-term plans, he has a five-step plan he calls "The L.E.S.I.R. Plan." You need to *Learn* what you need to learn, so you can *Earn* what you need to earn, so you can *Save* what you need to save, so that you can *Invest* what you need to invest, so that you can *Retire*, and do so being financially secure.

On the surface it seems a pretty simple plan. But unless one is dedicated to it, it is not. Jim stresses you have got to be intentionally focused on looking out after yourself today, *and* also looking out after yourself for the future.

"I can't be more clear on this. Beyond living up to today's responsibilities, unless you get run over by a concrete truck on your way home, you have a future. Some portion of every day needs to be devoted to building the foundation to that future. Choose your today's actions wisely!"

With that in mind, one of the first planning issues, encountered by many just starting out, is that of getting hired in the first place. That is a planning process in itself.

Dr. Jeffrey Magee is a recipient of the United States Guard Victory Award and the United States Junior Chamber of Commerce TOYA (Ten Outstanding Young Americans) Award. Dr. Jeff has been called one of today's leading "Leadership & Marketing Strategists." He works with C-Suite, Business Leaders, Military Generals, CEO2CEO Peer Groups across America, as well as with Governors, Congressional leaders... and the last three Presidents' of the United States.

Dr. Jeff has created a magazine called "Professional Performance Magazine," which is available on-line and as a hard copy subscription. He's a best-selling author of 21 books, including the popular best seller *Your Trajectory Code*. He is also a volunteer, advisory board member for the Young Eagle Entrepreneurs.

Dr. Jeff came to find when he was searching for a job that he needed to do some planning. He perceived that people were going to hire him for basically only four reasons. And he learned these the hard way. So, he knows this perspective is reliable. For that reason, he strongly urges people to always be working on these four reasons to be hired.

> "It doesn't matter if you're a high school student looking for your first job, you're a college aged student – whether you went to college or not – and in your late teens or early twenties, or really just any age. These four reasons will apply.

1. Accomplishments
2. Education and Credentials
3. Professional Body-of-Work and Subject-Matter-Expert (SME)
4. Income or Standard-of-Living Key Performance Indicator(s) of Achievement above and beyond the demographic of the average."

Dr. Jeff points out, number one, you are going to be hired because of what you have previously accomplished. Perspective employers are basically asking: What have you done; what have you accomplished from birth to this day that you are trying to get employed? A perspective employer wants to know what kind of knowledge and skill and abilities you can apply to his or her business.

He notes that if you're a high school or full-time college student and you've been having summer jobs or you have your own little small micro business on the side, that is a phenomenal story to share with a perspective employer. That experience can be put into a cover letter, or added appropriately in your resume, or during an interview, because that's a part of your previous body of work.

"Second, are your credentials. Credentials in terms of completed education. Do you have an Associate's degree, a Bachelor's degree, a Master's degree, a Doctorate's degree?

But it doesn't have to be just college. Have you attended a trade school? Are you an apprentice? Are you a journeyman? Do you have certifications? Do you have licenses? These are the many different ways employers can measure education.

That employer wants to confirm what's the level of education you have and if you've been previously part of an industry. If you have certifications, do you maintain them? *Are you accomplished?*

The third issue is identifying what you have specifically done in the profession to which you are applying. And what are your tangible measurements of success in this profession? What is your body-of-work professionally that you have learned, achieved, accomplished, and how are you seen within that framework as a Subject-Matter-Expert (SME)?

> "For me in the training world, as a subject matter expert, I would indicate the training courses I've done, the software, the books, the articles I've had published. I would indicate I've written books, 21 books to be exact, which have been translated into 23 different languages. These include college textbooks, as well as graduate-level management textbooks. And then there are the four best sellers."

The last issue is going to be indicating your income. It is one of the ways we all measure success, especially business people who are considering hiring you. So, what is the income you earn or what income do you generate off of your products. This is a Key Performance Indicator, a KPI.

A KPI is like a stepping stone, a marker, on a pathway. If you are on the right path, you'll step on each one going in the right direction. If you find you are stepping where there is not a stepping stone, you know you've taken a wrong turn. Plan accordingly!"

Having looked at some of the processes by which planning is done, a word on practicality would be timely here. For many, unlike as we've seen with Jim Vaughn and Dr. Jeff Magee, the discipline to plan does not come naturally.

Often, people will say they are more comfortable *improvising*, "flying by the seat of their pants," than taking the time and effort to lay out a concise, written order of procedure. Though it cannot be stressed enough a detailed plan is more often than not a life-saver, one should note an improvised plan *can* work.

Chris Cayer is a competitive intelligence specialist with almost 30 years of experience in the world of business. Coupled with this is his extensive training in corporate management. Chris' expertise is used to help organizations solve their most demanding difficulties. His clients have included major U.S. Federal departments, as well as state governments, major banks, aerospace technology firms, authors, radio hosts, business gurus, and well-known businesses like Proctor & Gamble and Johnson & Johnson.

Whether you need an industry revolutionized or an inexpensive way to promote your organization to millions of people every week, Chris has an innovative solution for multitudes of businesses around the world.

Such success had humble beginnings. Chris acknowledges he was always younger and smaller than his peers. This usually led them to underestimate Chris' desire to succeed. And he used that to his advantage, especially when all the odds appeared to be stacked against him.

The first job that he ever got was when he was in high school. It was with a call center for a local newspaper. It was common knowledge that everybody at that call center had been there for generations. It was *the* newspaper for the region.

His job at the call center was to get subscribers to renew, or, if they did not yet subscribe to get a new subscription. He was expected to work off of a "script," a prepared sales pitch. But, he noted, they hadn't changed the script for their phone calls in 25 or 30 years.

Worse, when a person got a call from the paper's sales representative it was usually at dinner time. There was no caller ID in those days, so the person wouldn't know who was calling. He or she would have to get up, leave the dinner table, and pick up the phone. Interrupting their dinner meant they would usually be angry. Within the first five words they knew exactly who it was and they would slam the phone down.

That was the work Chris would be doing. And, apart from the script, the training was basically non-existent. Except for his boss telling him to work the script. If he varied from it, he would be fired.

Also, at the end of every night, if he hadn't sold at least six subscriptions, he would be fired. That was it. "Get to work!"

Inevitably, he knew that at some point he was going to have a bad day – maybe even on his *first* day! Not surprisingly, they had a high turnover rate, which is why they had a job opening for a teenager.

Dutifully, he started on the phones. The next 45 minutes into the job were a disaster. He was getting nowhere with phones being slammed down in his ear. Or people telling him off. The script didn't work. Actually, people didn't even give him a chance to use the script.

It was a 4-hour shift and, soon, three had already blown by with only one subscription. There was no way of getting six. At that point, he made a big decision. Figuring he was going to be fired anyway, Chris decided to improvise: He changed the script.

> "I started calling everybody 'Bob.' As soon as the person picked up the phone I said, 'Hi, is this Mr. and Mrs. So-and-So?' 'Yep.' 'Thanks so much. Do you mind if I call you Bob? Thanks Bob, I appreciate it. I'm calling from such-and-such newspaper, Bob. Do you get the paper Bob?' The lady on the other end of the phone would be like, 'But my name's not Bob. It's Margaret.' I'd say, 'I know Margaret... I mean Bob. You see, I

talk to three to four hundred people a night. You're not going to remember my name – I'm not going to remember yours. I just make it easy and call everybody Bob. Thanks so much… Bob.'

"Then I would continue, 'Do you get the paper Bob?' There would be this 'Uh, well, no.' 'Do you like to cook, Bob?' 'Well yeah.' 'Did you know that there's $300 worth of coupons in there for all of your baking needs this week?' 'No, I didn't.' 'So Bob, can I sign you up for the paper?' 'Sure.' 'Let me have your credit card.' Done!

"I set records that night for the most number of subscriptions. I set records all summer long. By the end of it, they were trying to hire me as the Director of Sales for the call center. At 13-years old! I accepted, but had to quit two days later to go back to school."

Like Chris, inspiration can be immediate, on-the-spot. Keep in mind, however, that one's inspiration for planning can come from a number of different sources. Ken Rochon (Chapter 1) whose dad was career military, causing Ken to live most of his pre-teen years outside the United States, got his insight into planning from his readings.

Ken recalls he read a book when he was right around 12 or 13 years old. This was about the time he knew he wanted to be an entrepreneur. He still enthusiastically recommends this book to anyone in middle school. It's *The Adventures of Tom Sawyer* by Mark Twain.

The book, Ken acknowledges, taught him about the concept of "leverage," using what you have to "move" things along, get things done. In the story, there was a picket fence that needed to be painted. Instead of painting it all by himself, Tom Sawyer was able to convince his friends that painting the fence was an adventure. So, naturally he got them to *want* to paint the fence for him. Problem solved!

> "When I encountered my own problems in life I actually thought, 'What would Tom Sawyer do?' I think I became a Master Leverager because I never looked at life as I *have* to do this. I always looked at it as *how can I plan to get it done*!

> "I mean, if you look at him, Tom was a planner. He taught how life didn't have to be the way everyone else was doing it.

> "Take for example, if you look at the average kid today and you say, 'Hey, go ahead and paint this fence.' They're going to say, 'Okay how do I do it?' And it will probably take them 20 hours to accomplish it.

> "But a kid who plans will say to all the other kids on the block, 'Hey if you want pizza in my house' – he knows his mom's gonna buy pizza – 'grab a brush.' With everyone helping,

> the job gets done in an hour. He just saved 19
> hours of his life!"

The Ken Rochon-Tom Sawyer approach notwithstanding, it is important to understand, regardless of how you are inspired, regardless of whether you have pre-planned or improvised on-the-spot, regardless of how perfect your plans may appear, *inevitably* you will encounter resistance to them. This *adversity* shows up in many different forms.

5 ADVERSITY

One who gains strength by overcoming obstacles
possesses the only strength which can overcome adversity.

Albert Schweitzer

Ad-ver-si-ty *n.* a calamitous or disastrous
experience: MISFORTUNE.

One does not have to make an overt attempt at success to
encounter roadblocks, set-backs, fear of uncertainty, naysayers,
and failures. Life itself will throw these your way even if you
are a couch-potato. It is an unfortunate fact of life.

And, as an aside, it is ironical that those who spend a lifetime
of going out of their way to avoid these adversities, somehow
seem to encounter them all the more! Life indeed is not fair!

So, it is not surprising that those who risk, those who identify
and attempt to attain a goal, are also subject to these adversities.
It is almost an adage, if not a cliché, "To risk is to fail."

But, to the person driven to attain success, one failure is not
the end. What was the British poet, Alfred, Lord Tennyson's
line? "Better to have loved and lost, than never to have loved

at all." Tennyson knew the attempt was worth the trouble... and its possible failure!

And, so it is with the men and women who have gone before us... to success.

Because adversity is such a defining moment for an individual, so many people cave in and quit, it is important to see the many ways it is overcome.

One of the primary adversities we face is within ourselves: Fear. If not overcome, it can be paralyzing.

Dr. Len Schwartz is a former practicing chiropractor. He started his practice in 1993 and quickly built one of the largest practices in the Philadelphia region. He actually started his marketing company in 1999 to help other doctors and professionals automate their growth in their practices. Since then he has worked with, and partnered with, people like the late Chet Holmes, the late Jay Levinson, J.J. Abrams, Tony Robbins, Michael Gerber, and dozens of other internationally-known marketing and business building leaders.

Dr. Len is known for advising people, "If you want to double your leads, double your sales, and put simple systems into place in order to work with 25% to 50% less effort, then we should have a conversation together." He has systems and solutions in place that can help his clients achieve those successes.

Dr. Len is an expert in lead generation and automation so his clients can have more free time, more cash flow, and really relax more. He also owns one of the largest groups on LinkedIn called "Marketing and Networking for Doctors and Professionals" with almost 86,000 members! Further, he also has several marketing companies from which he provides doctors and professionals automated systems to help them build their practices and develop their marketing solutions.

Which raises the issue, how does one overcome the fear that often occurs in undertaking a new business venture (or any undertaking for that matter)?

Dr. Len finds that far too many people only act when they are in a state of absolute surety. They want a kind of complete certainty in order to take the next step.

He believes you should take a look at the most successful people; and he is not just talking about wealth, he means success in any endeavor. These successful people, at least, once in their rise to that success acted when there was *not* 100% certainty. Meaning they were not absolutely sure that they would reach the level of success that they were aiming for. Or any success at all.

But they acted anyway! They stepped out in faith expecting that one step would lead to the next step and the next step after that.

In Dr. Len's case, it would have been impossible for him to say he *knew* he was going to be where he is currently at now. He knows he could have never projected exactly where his business would be, almost 20 years later. He just knew that he had the power to help other people and knew he could help them in a big way.

Working off of that belief, he put one foot in front of the other, one day after the next. As they say, *one day at a time.*

By stepping out, things unfolded for him and opportunities came his way. People came into his life and as circumstances would have it, in different situations at different times one thing led to the other. The ball kept rolling and his business kept growing.

> "As I always say, 'one day at a time.' You've only got *this* day right now. You don't have tomorrow; you no longer have yesterday. All you have is right now, the present. So, you do the best that you possibly can in the here-and-now.

> "I'll take that one step further *now* and do whatever it takes to make that one step a success. That's what separates people who win and succeed at the highest possible level from those who don't. They are willing to take that necessary step… regardless of the risk. They are willing to put aside their fear and step out. It's the only way to get to the next level."

The second most-encountered adversity, and very common these days, is the adversity of criticism. One will almost certainly face those opposed to your goal when you step out to create something new. Most often this criticism comes in the form of a naysayer. This is someone who is in opposition to the very activity you are about to undertake, and criticizes you for even making the attempt.

hat you are doing – and *why* – you
ship, and diminish some of their
deepens the "wedge" between you
vay, initiating conversation, she has
th her family and misunderstanding
s notwithstanding.

ot outsiders, or personal family
accept or reject your business
commend you always still stay
d, I'm going to say it again,
have a strong enough "why," it
go forward.' Others don't have to
rder for you to be determined for
ss. *You* do. That is the reason I am
ed and passionate on my 'Why.'"

ry people closest to us become the biggest
ughn (Chapter 1) knows this firsthand. He
to deal with those who did not see his vision.
relate. As a result, they unknowingly, or, most
, became an obstacle.

ds that the people who are closest to you are
ggest naysayers. So, don't be surprised if this
u. He believes the reason why is that they don't
see. Because, most times they are not visionary;
possibly see the future as you do. And because they
hey think you're crazy.

that people accuse other people of being crazy
he accusers don't "hear the music." His own

A fitting example is Stephanie Frank whom we previously saw had a core value of "freedom" (Chapter 1). Her overwhelming success notwithstanding, there are still people who will criticize her! Criticism is, indeed, the bane of every entrepreneur.

Criticism, she notes, has come from the people that she knows and the people that she doesn't. So, Stephanie has her own two different answers for dealing with naysayers.

> "For the record, I've had gobs of haters and smear campaigns. I'm a very sensitive person and I'm very honest and authentic, so when somebody says something bad regardless, it hurts. It absolutely hurts because the practical answer would be, 'Oh, don't worry about it. It's just feedback. Deal with it.' The truth is – it does hurt. Even today I can still recall a bad review, from 12 years ago, in the midst of 120 good ones. It still hurts because that review did not accurately describe what had happened. Which just adds to the frustration."

Stephanie has found that a person has got to develop in such a way that he or she can maturely handle things like this. She knows from experience, if you're going to put yourself out there as an entrepreneur, or any venture for that matter, you should expect it.

She knows that if, over the years, you have developed, especially as a leader, you will find your greatest gift will be your ability to understand other people and their motivations. Again, you are attempting to answer the question "Why?" Why are they being critical?

Sometimes it is just personality. As noted before, Stephanie loves freedom and creativity. This can cause friction with those who prefer absolute, rigid structure. So, people who are more inclined towards that way of doing things are going to look at her as being not so credible, thus producing a negative reaction or response. She realizes this up-front in her dealings with them and is prepared for any negativity it might cause.

Learning this insight of personality differences over time has led her into the whole behavioral area of her work. She has come to realize that everyone acts from their own set of values – their motivators – whether *they* are aware of it or not. Thus, their criticism is always coming from their point of view. Again, which may not be hers. Though this understanding doesn't totally remove the emotional response of being hurt, she understands it is helpful in preventing one from retaliating.

> "There is that famous old saying, 'You know your opinion of me is none of my business.' I have that on my wall as a reminder. It really is none of your business what other people think of you, especially those people that don't know you. It's just their opinion – really, their *guess* – not a fact.
>
> "The truth is, if you're running a business, not everybody is going to like you. That's just the way it is. Be mature enough to live with it if you are going to take on the responsibility of being a business owner."

If you share with them w
can deepen the relation
misgivings. Silence just
both. In doing it this
always gotten along wi
friends, their misgiving

"Whether or
and friends,
interests, I r
focused. A
'When you
makes you
like it in o
your succe
very focus

Sometimes the v
naysayers. Jim V
consistently had
They could not
likely, *knowing*

He understan
usually the b
happens to y
see what you
they cannot
don't see it,

Jim muses
because t

p
hi
not

Rega
more t
someth
and isn't
might be
risk of jea

Then there i
what you are
entrepreneur, a
you're constant
looks strange to

And as a business
members who have
here's how life works
you graduate from sc
school, you get marri
can then go on to have
traditional view.

The way she has dealt w
responsibility, she feels, is h
doing, you then have contro
how you react to any of their

A fitting example is Stephanie Frank whom we previously saw had a core value of "freedom" (Chapter 1). Her overwhelming success notwithstanding, there are still people who will criticize her! Criticism is, indeed, the bane of every entrepreneur.

Criticism, she notes, has come from the people that she knows and the people that she doesn't. So, Stephanie has her own two different answers for dealing with naysayers.

> "For the record, I've had gobs of haters and smear campaigns. I'm a very sensitive person and I'm very honest and authentic, so when somebody says something bad regardless, it hurts. It absolutely hurts because the practical answer would be, 'Oh, don't worry about it. It's just feedback. Deal with it.' The truth is – it does hurt. Even today I can still recall a bad review, from 12 years ago, in the midst of 120 good ones. It still hurts because that review did not accurately describe what had happened. Which just adds to the frustration."

Stephanie has found that a person has got to develop in such a way that he or she can maturely handle things like this. She knows from experience, if you're going to put yourself out there as an entrepreneur, or any venture for that matter, you should expect it.

She knows that if, over the years, you have developed, especially as a leader, you will find your greatest gift will be your ability to understand other people and their motivations. Again, you are attempting to answer the question "Why?" Why are they being critical?

Sometimes it is just personality. As noted before, Stephanie loves freedom and creativity. This can cause friction with those who prefer absolute, rigid structure. So, people who are more inclined towards that way of doing things are going to look at her as being not so credible, thus producing a negative reaction or response. She realizes this up-front in her dealings with them and is prepared for any negativity it might cause.

Learning this insight of personality differences over time has led her into the whole behavioral area of her work. She has come to realize that everyone acts from their own set of values – their motivators – whether *they* are aware of it or not. Thus, their criticism is always coming from their point of view. Again, which may not be hers. Though this understanding doesn't totally remove the emotional response of being hurt, she understands it is helpful in preventing one from retaliating.

> "There is that famous old saying, 'You know your opinion of me is none of my business.' I have that on my wall as a reminder. It really is none of your business what other people think of you, especially those people that don't know you. It's just their opinion – really, their *guess* – not a fact.

> "The truth is, if you're running a business, not everybody is going to like you. That's just the way it is. Be mature enough to live with it if you are going to take on the responsibility of being a business owner."

Stephanie also sees where people get into the trap of trying to make *everybody* like them. She calls it "pulling the boulder up the hill." Why would you want to do that when you have people running alongside of you going, "Hey, let's get up the hill together." These are good people who are pulling for you, not against you.

Regarding people who personally know her, that is a little more tricky. And a bit more difficult. Especially if you're doing something that another person in your life seriously wants and isn't able to achieve themselves. She knows that rejection might be nothing more than jealousy. And there is *always* the risk of jealousy.

Then there is the person who just flat-out doesn't understand what you are doing, or want what you want to do. As an entrepreneur, as an inventor, or whatever you're willing to try, you're constantly putting yourself out there into a world that looks strange to a whole lot of people.

And as a business*woman*, Stephanie had a lot of her family members who have very staunch views on success. She observes, here's how life works for them: You grow up, you go to school, you graduate from school, you get honors, you go to graduate school, you get married, you have a family. With *that*, you can then go on to have a job or run a business. It is *the* very traditional view.

The way she has dealt with this, is to speak to them. The responsibility, she feels, is hers – *you* have to initiate. But in so doing, you then have control – and freedom of choice – over how you react to any of their opposition.

If you share with them what you are doing – and *why* – you can deepen the relationship, and diminish some of their misgivings. Silence just deepens the "wedge" between you both. In doing it this way, initiating conversation, she has always gotten along with her family and misunderstanding friends, their misgivings notwithstanding.

> "Whether or not outsiders, or personal family and friends, accept or reject your business interests, I recommend you always still stay focused. And, I'm going to say it again, 'When you have a strong enough "why," it makes you go forward.' Others don't have to like it in order for you to be determined for your success. *You* do. That is the reason I am *very* focused and passionate on my 'Why.'"

Sometimes the very people closest to us become the biggest naysayers. Jim Vaughn (Chapter 1) knows this firsthand. He consistently had to deal with those who did not see his vision. They could not relate. As a result, they unknowingly, or, most likely, *knowingly*, became an obstacle.

He understands that the people who are closest to you are usually the biggest naysayers. So, don't be surprised if this happens to you. He believes the reason why is that they don't see what you see. Because, most times they are not visionary; they cannot possibly see the future as you do. And because they don't see it, they think you're crazy.

Jim muses that people accuse other people of being crazy because the accusers don't "hear the music." His own philosophy is, if you can hear the music – dance and enjoy yourself! Even if you dance alone.

The people who have been negative about his goals, dreams, and ambitions in life were the individuals who may have loved him with all of their heart, but their goals, dreams, and ambitions, if they had any at all, were completely different than his own.

And though they love you, he notes, and you love them, you have to "turn them off" and stop listening to their negativity.

The antidote to those kinds of negative thinkers is to seek out individuals who are already doing what you want to do. *They* will be a positive influence. Especially if they have been *very* successful. As you learn what they have achieved, and how they achieved it, you will find you are getting all the support that you need.

So long as you understand this, you'll realize it is wiser to not spend a whole lot of time with people who are negative thinkers. The ones who are always telling you, 'It'll never fly.' Jim knows if you spend enough time with them, whatever you are trying to accomplish will indeed "never fly."

There are always people who want to get into your head to prevent your success. Jim sees that if your *thinking* is not right, your *doing* is not going to be right. And you're not going to end up with what you want in life.

He has found that each person is the gatekeeper of his or her own mind. You need to be diligent to safeguard it at all times. So, he cautions, stop listening to those in opposition. If they have something negative to say, move on and find better people.

> "I have a great quote from one of the most successful persons ever, Andrew Carnegie, claimed by many to have been the richest man in history: 'The greatest gift the creator gave you at birth was the power to take control of your own mind and direct it to any end result you desire.'
>
> "Taking that advice, don't let the naysayers prevent you from achieving *your* desire."

Jessica Peterson (Chapter 2) has had similar experiences dealing with those who were opposed to her vision. She also has found sometimes those who have been in opposition have been family members. This can, she notes, cause one to put up a response of self-defense: 'How dare they say that?'

But, she has found that if she steps back for a moment, she realizes that, for family members or friends, it just comes from a place of love. Love, even when they might become more forceful, like sometimes she has had family members *demand* that she obey them. At that point, she politely lets them know she appreciates their input and will consider it.

And though a family member may voice an opinion, it does not mean she has to listen or act on it. She finds that if she disagrees, it is best to just smile and let it go.

Again, she is respectful; "they are family after all." But, at the same time, she knows where she is going and what she is doing. What is the adage? *Take it with a grain of salt.*

However, she does advise that if there are people in your life who are always putting you down, it may be time to evaluate if it's time to let them go.

> "It reminds me of advice I once received from a woman I know; I think it is also from a book: We're all in charge of our own bus. People get on our bus at the right time and people get off at the right time. But sometimes we need to kick them off the bus. And we need to be savvy enough to do just that and let them go when they have worn out their welcome.
>
> "The truth is, the only time someone can really affect you, is if you allow them to rent space in your head.
>
> "Life's too short to deal with the other people. A lot of naysayers really don't care for you. Let's be honest and realistic about that, and realize it's time to let them go. I mean, haters hate and there's going to be haters out there."

Jessica also notes that when you're growing and developing, there's going to be people that get jealous. People that covet your success. They get jealous and often out of spite they come off negative.

To overcome this, she believes that if you are confident and know who you are and what your purpose is, there's going to be people out there who are actually going to support you. She advises, "Those people you keep!"

Bob Holmes, who grew up in the Boston, MA area, is known as "The One-Man Volleyball Team." He, literally, plays as one man against an entire, opposing volleyball team!

As an adult, Bob did a lot of traveling, which caused him to develop a bad back. His doctor recommended that he get more exercise. It was at that time Bob began playing volleyball with a friend from church in their back yard. He played 3 or 4 times a week, usually after evening programs.

After watching the famed Globetrotters entertain a crowd, and seeing the joy they brought to young people, he came up with the idea of a one-man volleyball team. He would use that unique sports venue to demonstrate to people that they can beat the odds just as he was doing on the court. Here were the beginnings of his "Beat The Odds" message.

Since then his compassion for others keeps him on the road traveling across the country. His One-Man Volleyball Team has been in over 5,000 gymnasiums in front of a total of over 3.5-million people! At each venue, Bob is helping the youth of our country see that they *can* "Beat the Odds." When his One-Man Volleyball team passes off this earth, Bob wants the epitaph on his tombstone to read: "It wasn't the Volleyball, but the Message that kept me going."

Because of his very unique means of employment, Bob has had to deal with his fair share of naysayers. However, he sees it not so much as naysaying, but rather as just being misunderstood.

> "Most of my encounters with those who are skeptical are the result of their misunderstanding. Once they see the heart of what I do, and hear me speak, that whole thing changes.

> "Here's a few examples: One guy when he heard *One-Man Volleyball Team* thought I played against myself; that I ran back and forth under the net playing both sides. Somebody else thought I played against the wall.

> "But, when they came to the event and found out that I was playing against from six or more opposing players… and by myself, their attitude changed.

> "And remember, this is on a court the same size that a whole team would have played on. Their attitude definitely changed when they saw me *beat* the other team!"

So, how does one deal with naysayers? Chris Salem (Chapter 3), who we saw wasn't going to allow his high school sports coach to dictate his hair length, has a solid insight into dealing with this opposition?

"The first thing to do is to set boundaries. I make it a point to not allow a naysayer to penetrate my way of thinking. You can't successfully live the life other people want you to live. It just can't be done.

"I'm not trying to become Mr. Right to everybody. I'd rather be living my life's purpose than making every naysayer happy.

"Therefore, if you have to detach yourself from a negative person, then you have to do that. The key is that you live your life for who you are. You have to make the choices necessary to live *your* purpose. Then the people who see what you are doing, and believe in what you are doing, those are the people who you want around you.

"Finally, like with a mentor, surround yourself with people that are the same. That is going to keep you grounded and keep you thinking positively. I can guarantee that you will be easily derailed if you constantly hang around the naysayers."

Chris Cayer (Chapter 4), adds to this insight. He has a perspective, which he developed from his own many negative experiences. It is a very powerful mental exercise, and one he walks people through to guide them towards their own success in overcoming opposition.

He observes that when those naysayers get in your head, it can be very depressing. In the extreme, it can cause you to lose all hope. Especially when the people you believe should be supporting you turn out to be not really on your team. With them especially, it feels like betrayal.

In those instances, you can quickly view it as if there's nobody left for you; you are absolutely on your own. If everybody's only spreading doom and gloom around you, sooner or later that rubs off, and that's what gets in your head.

He firmly believes that the saying is true, "You are the sum total of the five people most frequently in your life." If every one of them is telling you negative things about you, what your plans are, what you're trying to do in regards to your business, your head space is going to get filled with that negativity.

Chris has developed a method to deal with all of this. He calls it the *Wish Program*. It is the result of years of his own personal dealing with dreadful input. And the idea behind it is really straightforward.

He suggests that you imagine that you walked out your front door and you tripped over this little clump of brass sticking out of the ground. It annoyed you and you didn't want anybody else to trip over it, so you took the time to dig it up. But, doing that now has made you late.

Being late now has made you really pretty cranky. Nonetheless, you dust off the clump of brass. Come to find out it's Aladdin's lamp. With your rubbing, *Poof*, out comes this all-powerful genie.

The genie tells you he is going to grant you three wishes, but there are some rules. You can't bring anybody back from the dead. You can't make anybody fall in love with you. You can't kill anybody. And especially, no more wishing for more wishes.

Then the genie throws in a clunker: Whatever you wish for he intends to make it work against you. He will do this by following *exactly* – to the letter – the words you use to describe the wish to him.

With that fair warning, he advises he will be back in a week to start granting your wishes. In the meantime, you have to take that time to really idiot-proof those wishes. Because otherwise, they are going to come back and bite you.

The genie then clearly makes it known he guarantees it. With that, *Poof,* the genie goes away.

"Oh great," you think, now you have that sense often found in a normal depressive environment; that things are really stacked against you. Yet, at the same time, everything you have *ever* wanted is within your reach. You have what has to be *the* complete paradox right in front of you. How do you resolve this?

> "It is all in perspective. If you see that the genie represents hope, there's a chance that you can make this work after all. That hope leads you to want to develop a step-by-step plan to counter any ill-effects the genie might throw at you. You are, literally, designing what you need to do to make the Wish

happen… without the genie harming you in the process!

"If you devote enough time to it, you really do see enough of the pitfalls to be able to counter them. At this point, you begin to see opportunities and openings to be able to go do what it is you really want to accomplish.

"It's the same with those who are opposed to what you want to do. Their opposition should cause you to dig and plan more thoroughly, which leads to your success. Like the genie, they then are not a hindrance, but a help. They motivate you to be better prepared.

"And all of this begins with hope. It's very hard for any obstruction to prevent you from accomplishing what you want to accomplish when you continually have hope."

Whether opposition is fear, naysayers, or some other form of resistance, Eric Lofholm (Chapter 2), whose business-calling we saw began with his sports card sales in high school, has a final word on the subject. It is a very practical insight that needs to be acknowledged.

He advises to always take action in the face of resistance. The purpose of the action is not necessarily for the resistance to go away. It's that a person takes action to force his or her way *through* the resistance. Eric knows this is effective because of the many times he has faced resistance.

Where most people fail, he observes, is on an unconscious level. There, once they feel any resistance, they then just stop. This happens a lot when starting a business or other venture.

Eric relates this to how he felt when he left employment with Tony Robbins. His resistance was his own self-inflicted fear of failure.

To push past that fear, he determined that if the business failed, then he would just go back and get a sales job. In pushing ahead then, taking action by starting his business, he would actually be no further behind. He figured his worst-case scenario was that he was right back where he started.

In this way, he felt he had no risk. This helped him push through any fear. It gave him the courage to start even though he was, initially, very afraid.

He noted, this pushing forward can become even more demanding when you've encountered failure. Much like his first business in 1995, which failed miserably. That venture only lasted about four months.

> "I went out of business and it caused a lot of trauma in my life; it caused a lot of trauma in my marriage. That's when I even went through a bankruptcy. Those, and more, were all things that came out of my first company failing.
>
> "A few years later, I wanted to start up another company. But, the last time I did this, the whole world fell apart. What if I failed again?

"Having survived one major failure led me to believe I could survive another. My attitude was, 'I'll just go get another job - it's no big deal.'

"With that attitude, I just stepped out and did it!"

Eric demonstrated that this is the difference between successful individuals and those who are not. The accomplished person "steps out and does it," while others slink back in fear and do not.

So, whether the naysayer is a family member, a friend, an enemy, or yourself, to be successful you must continue to focus on what you intend to accomplish and not be swayed from attaining it.

Which leads to the next key to success. Over the years successful person, after successful person has acknowledged there is one element of their character that is absolutely necessary for overcoming adversity and going on to success. It is that of personal *discipline*.

6   DISCIPLINE

Discipline is the bridge between goals... and accomplishment.

Jim Rohn

Dis-ci-pline *n.* training that perfects mental
faculties or moral character: SELF-CONTROL.

More often than not, the word *discipline* is seen as the practice
of training people to obey rules or a code of behavior, and,
failing that, using punishment to correct disobedience. Ask
almost any parent... or anyone who has served in the military.
This concept of punishment, however, often applies in relation
to the disciplining imposed on others; as a parent punishing
an unruly child, or a drill sergeant "educating" a new recruit!

But for those who intend to push on to success, the discipline
needed doesn't come from an outsider; it is *self*-imposed
discipline. Self-discipline will, as Jim Rohn so perfectly noted,
be necessary to bridge the gap between current reality and
one's future goals. That discipline, self-discipline, allows us to
actually attain those goals.

One key element of self-discipline is that it provides one with
the ability to control his or her feelings. This very often is

necessary to overcome one's weaknesses, such as anger... or slothfulness. It is also linked to the issue of perseverance, which we looked at in the previous chapter in relation to adversity. And discipline is especially necessary in regards to the ability of pursuing what one thinks is right... despite temptations to abandon that pursuit.

Self-discipline can be described as an "invisible magic." None of your five senses can detect it, but its effects are life-changing. Those who exercise it can take their natural talents to even greater heights. Self-discipline can even take a *lack* of natural talent and implant that talent in you propelling one to success.

There are a number of ways to develop self-discipline. We will look at five as a starting point.

First, you should rarely decide to do something based on whether it *feels* good or not. Most roads to success require a *have*-to-do, not a *want*-to-do. Though our culture instills the perspective that "if it feels good, it is right," the truth is, that viewpoint will most often lead to disaster. By doing what is *required*, even if we are "not in the mood," is the essence of self-discipline.

Coupled with this is the need to quit inventing excuses. An excuse is the lie you tell yourself (and others) to get out of doing the have-to. If you are not honest with yourself, how can you be honest with others? Developing excuses as a way of life is a character trait you want to avoid at all costs. The time spent on whining could be used by you to further your success instead.

Once you've overcome your inertia (and excuses) to do nothing, the next aspect comes into play: You need to complete what you start. The cliché "Quitters are losers" holds consistently true. If it was important enough for you to begin, as an act of honor, it should be important enough to bring it to a close.

Don't misunderstand. Not everything in life we attempt is successful. There are times when it is wisest to "cut the bait." But, if you are consistently starting projects that you never complete, this is an issue of character, not an issue of your "circumstances." And, your chances for future success diminish with each incomplete undertaking: Failure begets failure. The best advice that can be offered here is be willing to respect your own self enough to fulfill the promise of success you made to yourself when you began.

The next follows "as night, the day,": Don't get sidetracked. In today's world, with iPhones, Internet, and television, we can too quickly get drawn away from each required have-to. Be on guard that you don't get "skyjacked" by all these electronic detours. Or by anything else that is trivial and a distraction to pursuing your goals.

Self-discipline is the means to overcoming these diversions. By staying focused you will not only achieve your goal(s), but also develop self-respect, which will greatly improve your mental well-being.

The last is a *method* of self-discipline. Every goal or project can be broken down into "bite-sized" pieces. No matter how large, or how complex, every goal or project is a composite of its separate parts. Learn to develop the ability to break down the "whole" into its individual components. And then make each one into an achievable step. From there, develop each have-to, *and then do that which is required*. This will lead to a successful completion of each step. And then plan and do the next one. The outcome is your *complete* success!

One of the first places, outside of the home, we begin to learn self-discipline is in school. School work, *homework*, requires it! Dr. Len Schwartz (Chapter 5), whom we saw encourage that "one step" necessary to overcome adversity, also saw the need for discipline in his school work to succeed.

If you asked him, Dr. Len would admit he had not been a great student in high school. He would say he was a good student, average. But, he knows he wasn't living up to his potential.

Dr. Len really loved playing sports. He would much rather play sports than really study hard. In this way he got away with "B's" instead of the "A's" he might have gotten had he really applied himself. But at the time, he was satisfied with that. He knows he could have done better.

It was the knowledge of that potential which, for as long as he could remember, caused him to want to be a doctor. He was so sure he would be, he actually used to practice his signature. He did this as early as third and fourth grade, for that one day when he would become a doctor and have to sign prescriptions.

His practicing his prescription signature, notwithstanding, every counselor he met from elementary, to middle, and especially high school, would tell him to choose another career path. They were always polite... but serious. Without good grades, they knew he would never get into medical school.

> "As I remember, I was a sophomore and I met
> with my college guidance counselor. During

one of our meetings he came out and told me, 'You know, I've got to be honest with you. I just don't see this career path of "doctor" as happening for you.'

"That was a defining moment for me. I knew I was capable, but every person, teacher, advisor, every counselor looked at my grades and said, 'No way!' In fact, there was my chemistry teacher in high school who told me I shouldn't even bother applying to *college*, much less medical school.

"I think, collectively, this ultimately just strengthened me. Finally, hearing all the 'no-you-cannots' made me sit up and listen.

"Either I was going to fold up, pack it in, and do something else… or I needed to create a Plan B and buckle-down. I decided I was going to stay the course, have faith in myself, and actually accomplish what I knew I was capable of."

Dr. Len would eventually get accepted to Penn State. There, he would discover his calling to be a chiropractor. This caused him to further commit, "buckle down," to studying.

Due to the applied self-discipline of study, Dr. Len would go on to graduate and become a chiropractor. In fact, he eventually built up one of the largest chiropractic practices in the Philadelphia area. If an educational route is needed for your success, as it was with Dr. Len, the discipline of study is not an option.

There is also another avenue of "learning" discipline. Dr. Will Moreland (Chapter 3), whom we saw had joined the U.S. Army during an outing to his local mall, reflected on the principles of discipline he gained in the U.S. military.

> "I did six years of active duty, and two years in the reserves, eventually rising to the rank of Staff Sergeant (E-6). But, first things first.

> "Very quickly the Army provided structure for me. That structure provided the discipline necessary for success. That discipline was the gateway through which I would associate myself with good habits.

> "Through that discipline, I began to think long-term, probably for the first time in my life. It was here in the military, where I saw discipline was leading me to a structured life, that I began to have a real vision *for* my life.

> "That structure and discipline would provide me with an understanding of how to manage my time. This would lead to successfully completing my future education once I decided to undertake it. This developed the discipline of commitment, to actually accomplish the tasks set before me.

"Being in the military, and its resulting discipline, is when my life really started to transform and change. That developed self-discipline can be seen today in all of my current success."

Paul Hoyt (Chapter 3), who showed us that there can be multiple crossroads in our lives, would agree; discipline is transforming. He is convinced that discipline is a major trait of every super achiever.

One of the things that he does every day when he gets up in the morning, is that he writes what he calls the "energy of the day." He makes it a point to write something a little inspirational or insightful using a positive word that he chooses at random. As a result of this discipline, he has created, over the years, a list of 1,500 positive words.

He believes the power of this discipline has provided him with a tremendous sense of self-control. That discipline gives him a real sense of empowerment in his life.

"If you don't have some level of personal discipline in your life, I strongly recommend that you do something similar. It will send a message to you every single morning that you are in control. That will lead to the belief that you can accomplish this day's goals and overcome this day's challenges.

"When you focus on that and it sinks in deep, deep into your subconscious mind, it gives you a really expanded sense of control and empowerment. There's freedom in discipline."

Discipline has practical applications that are sometimes not always as self-evident as they are for Paul Hoyt. Dr. Jeff Magee (Chapter 4), whose guidelines we saw are a foundation for gaining employment, noted that to be successful he had to take calculated risks. With those risks come the fear of the unknown: Will it all work out as planned? The self-discipline of being willing to commit to decision-making, when others attempt to avoid it, helped overcome those concerns.

A number of years ago IBM came to Dr. Jeff. In their business model they had a sales side and an engineering side. And they were having a hard time getting the two entities to communicate with each other. As a result, they were getting bogged down because necessary decisions were not being made. This was causing them to lose market share.

Representatives from IBM approached Dr. Jeff because he had a reputation for being able to take big concepts and make them very simple. In this way companies could work through their problems and solve them. IBM wanted an uncomplicated way for their corporate departments to make decisions.

That's when he came up with the STOP™ Method. Which he now has been using for decades. He finds it especially good for not only decision-making, but also for launching into business, or other venture, unknowns. It guides a person to a continuous re-evaluation of his or her decisions to obtain a better return on investment (ROI).

Simply put, before you make a decision, you have to S-T-O-P it. Dr. Jeff notes that psychology confirms this method. It tells us that there are four things your brain wants before it makes any decision. Dr. Jeff's method addresses each.

In guiding individuals through that method, he advises to take a blank sheet of paper and just write out the word S-T-O-P. But do it *vertically*.

> "The 'S' stands for *stop and seek*: What is the problem? The issue? The need? The concern? The challenge? What is the opportunity? What is the stimulant here, the driving force moving this issue? This step answers the *what*.

> "The 'T' is for *target and think through 'why.'* Why is this a concern to you? Why should you care? Why are you getting involved? Why has it come to you? Why should you consider this; or better yet, why should you *not* do anything on this? This is an analytic step and it answers the question *why*.

> "The 'O' stands for *organized options*. How do I fix this? How do I resolve it? How do I eliminate it? How do I avoid it? If I can't resolve the issue, how do I cope with it so it doesn't debilitate my activities?

> "Last is the 'P.' I'll have a little fun here. People who are able to deal with fear effectively and work through the issue and become

successful are people who know-how to 'P.'
In fact, successful people 'P' everywhere.
Unsuccessful people don't know how to 'P'
anywhere.

"The key to 'P' is found in 'O,' in the work
'options,' which is plural. Options, plural, are
your insurance policy. You have to provide at
least two options before you move forward.
I need to say that again: You have to have at
least two options before you act.

"How do you know one idea is the best
if you don't have anything to compare it
with? So, that's why you 'P' – you *push* –
to get at least a second option. What often
happens, by pushing for that second option,
synergistically you create maybe an even
better third or fourth one. With multiple
options you now choose the best… and move
forward. At this point, don't procrastinate.
Act on your best option."

One can easily see it takes discipline to S-T-O-P and not
rush into an important decision. Those less disciplined, those
who will act in haste, will probably face a less than desirable
outcome.

All of this leads to the conclusion, which cannot be stressed
enough, discipline is a character trait that most definitely
separates those who are successful from those who are not.
Long term success depends on it. Yes, there are some who

succeed without it, but more often than not, that success is short-lived.

A fitting example of this can be seen in many famous sports personalities. Almost a cliché these days, those once-famous individuals who lacked the self-discipline necessary to safeguard their enormous income, find themselves later in trouble. Years after their "retirement" (sometimes just a few short years), they wind up penniless. They lacked the self-discipline for long-term success by squandering their once enormous stockpile of money.

Don't you be like them! Develop self-discipline in order to guide you to – and safeguard – your success.

7   SELLING

If people like you, they'll listen to you,
but if they trust you, they'll do business with you.

Zig Zigler

Sell-ing v. persuade someone the merits of: PROMOTE.

For most people, the idea of *sales* usually conjures up the pushy person who is rapping at your front door, or giving you that unsolicited phone call, at the worst possible moment.

But, if you were attending a class in economics, you would be taught that a *sales* was the last step in the chain of commerce where a buyer exchanges cash for a seller's goods or services. It is also referred to as the activity to bring this exchange about, as is in Zig Zigler's quote above.

The economic definition is important if your business *is* sales. The more general definition, however, provided in the first paragraph, is how most people see "sales."

As we saw previously with the college-hopeful person, he or she is actually selling him- or herself in the sense of trying to promote the benefit of them attending the school to which they are applying.

So, although many of the testimonies you are about to read are, in fact, sales in the economic sense, the idea of promotion expressed herein can be applied in other areas.

As a businessman, Chris Salem (Chapter 3) relates what sales are to his organizations. He knows that sales are extremely important. They are the life blood of any company. It's what brings the revenue in. But it is more than that. Sales are what delivers the message and the solution to somebody's, or some company's, problems. It solves their challenges.

The most important lesson he sees for sales as a profession is learning the ability to connect, and not so much "pitch." When you're able to connect with each human being, they are going to sense this energy that you're authentic, you're genuine, you're somebody they can trust. That can be a Chief Executive Officer, a Vice President, or another vital person in a tactical role. Once you're able to connect with them, they accept you as a means to their solution, not a "pushy salesperson."

He notes that the second most important step is to learn how to listen. And not just "hear" – *really listen*. Not only listen to the words they say, but observe their body language, observe the energy that's coming from them, and begin to really seek out where their problems, or their challenges, are.

When that has been revealed, the next action is to *not* jump into how to solve their problem. The next step is to inquire if you have their permission to offer a recommendation. They should now realize you're not attempting force; they are still in control. This further strengthens the bond being developed. At this point they should want to hear how you can potentially help them.

> "This applies to direct sales as well. I'm a firm believer people want to buy, but they want to make the decision to buy. They don't want to be 'sold.' You could have the greatest product or service on the face of the earth, and perhaps that *could* solve their problem, but they're not going to buy if you're doing everything that pushes them away. Like coming across as if you are forcing the issue."

Yet, there were times when sales were challenging for Chris. Notwithstanding, he always considered following a code of ethics, one that came from integrity, honesty, and being genuine.

As an example, in some instances during a meeting with a potential client he saw during preliminary discussions that, for some reason, his solution didn't seem to fit. It might be the right solution… but just not here in the current circumstances. In those instances, where he realized he could not effectively solve their problem, he would not attempt the sale.

Often he would then refer them to somebody else who he knew could better solve their issue. When that happened, and especially if the referred company helped them be successful, even though his company didn't benefit, the client he referred came to respect him.

> "They often remembered that selfless integrity, and if a future issue arose, they would reach out to see if I could help them with the new issue. If nothing else, they would be a great referral base because they took notice I was someone who put them first and was looking out for their best interest."

Similarly, over the years Chris Cayer (Chapter 4) has learned a lot about all aspects of business. One of the most important lessons, a lesson in reality, has been in regards to sales.

He views sales as being equivalent to what food is to the body. For him, sales are food for your business. If you don't feed your business enough, it's going to starve. So, sales are as important as food in your life.

But, he muses, you don't need to eat 24 hours a day, seven days a week. You must, however, eat regularly, otherwise you will starve. And you need a good blend of different foods, a variety, otherwise you can easily be vitamin-deficient. You need a variety.

> "Warren Buffet talked about having multiple streams of revenue. This is the fundamental part – you have to have a variety of anything in life. If you have only a one source in sales, and that turns off, you're definitely done."

Yes, selling itself can be a stark reality if that is your business. But, the sales concepts can be applied not only in the transaction of a product or a service. It really is a component of life. It hinges on who you are and with whom you have a working or friendly relationship. A relationship that is building *trust*.

Having been involved in sales, beginning in his teen years, Eric Lofholm (Chapter 2) offered what he considered the most important lesson about sales.

> "Selling is a learned skill anybody can learn. It's a set of principles that has nothing to do with what you're born with, skill-set wise. Some people are born more persuasive than others, but anybody can learn to sell successfully. For me, knowing that thought is very empowering.

> "There are several very successful trainers out there: Tom Hopkins, Brian Tracy, Dr. Moines, and myself. If you choose to go out and get professional training in sales, it's going to change your life for the better.

> *"Selling shows up in all of your relationships.* It shows up in your parenting, your personal relationships, in your business, and your joint ventures, amongst others. Your life is going to go a heck of a lot easier if you get professionally trained in sales.

> "It will probably take you six to twelve months – a real study to learn it. But once you have it, you have it for the rest of your life."

Jim Vaughn (Chapter 1) would agree. Selling is more than pushing a good or service. And you don't need a college degree to be successful at it.

Jim understands that people who learn trade skills which allowed them to be able to see and solve a problem, start a business, or sell their solutions on a grand scale, can be successful... worldwide. The required skills for success involves a solid knowledge in your chosen trade, the ability to overcome challenges, and, regardless of the career path, becoming proficient at what you do.

He offers a word of caution here: Regardless of how great a problem solver you are, unless you also know how to *sell* the solution, no one will even care about your "super resolution."

Nothing, he observes, ever happens until... Somebody... Somewhere... Sells... something to someone. And because a person's work is "worth his or her hire," that "sale" should be at some profitable price. Only then, do all the other jobs that support the sale become necessary.

> "Consider: if you have a job, it was because someone in sales made known the need for your talents to support your company's business efforts. Even government jobs are dependent on this 'sales success' in private enterprise. Without the profits from non-government entities, there would be nothing to tax. Without taxes, there is nothing to pay its workers. Government would cease to exist."

Coach A.M. Williams (Chapter 2), whose illness spurred him on to establish his own business, sees the issue of selling as being in a person's character.

> "Character and integrity. Don't promise what you can't do... and do everything you promised. Some people say 'under-promise, over-deliver.' I say '*fully* promise and over deliver.'

> "I mean, if you've been diagnosed with a disease and then been told you might have less than three months to live, do you want a doctor to under-promise and say, 'I don't know – I mean – I *might* be able to do something about it'? Or do you want him to say, 'I specialize and this is my specialty, so I *can* provide'?

> "Now we know ultimately there are no guarantees, but I let my clients know the reasons why they should want to do business with me instead of someone else. I let them know exactly what I can do for them, how I'm going to help them. I give them referrals of people that I have been successful with. People who have experienced 30-, 50-, 75-percent increase within a matter of a few months.

> "So, I strongly recommend that you want to fully-promise and over-deliver. Full of promise, because that's what makes you

different from everybody else. This whole notion of under-promising in order to make people think that you're giving them more because they got more than promised? I don't believe in that.

"If you can deliver the goods, you're a specialist. Then you fully-promise and you over-deliver. You over-deliver to the degree that they think they should have been paying you more because you gave them 10 times the value of what you said you would do, i.e., over-deliver what you actually took in payment. I'm a firm believer that if you do that enough, you become a trusted advisor and people will *want* you to be their consultant."

Ken Rochon (Chapter1) also sees the issue of sales as being established from relationships that are developed. He approaches sales from a social perspective. In his view, he is really trying to solve a problem that the customer has.

For Ken, this is truly the culminating success of sales. If you can prove that you are able to solve a lot of other persons' problems – and it's helpful to have testimonials or endorsements from your previous successes – then you have the easiest sales process. To the perspective customer you're a problem solver, not some demanding salesperson, and they're just paying you to solve their problem.

Also, he observes, money will not necessarily be the first thing in their decision making. It'll be more about you solving their problem that's right now *costing* them money. Or in business, you're going to solve a problem that's going to gain for them greater income. If you can't address these as solutions for your customer, or at least make known to them their liability can be made lower, then any of your sales are probably going to be a challenge.

Further, he feels that a person really has to have the right view of sales. He believes the word "sales" is a very beautiful word when you consider it. If, however, you look at sales as if it's a dirty word, then you're *not* going to approach it as customer *service*.

You have to look at sales as building a long-term relationship. You're there to help the customer over the long-haul. You are his or her problem-solver. And you'll work with them for as long as it takes to actually solve their problem. In this way, you are *helping* a fellow human being.

> "And when you solve their problem, they don't only give you money for your service, but they often want to endorse you to other people. And *that* is part of the long-term relationship."

As you can clearly see, sales are always linked to *relationships*.

8   RELATIONSHIPS

Personal relationships are the fertile soil
from which all advancement, all success,
all achievement in real life, grows

Ben Stein

Re-lat-tion-ship *n.* the state of being mutually
interacting in agreement: CONNECTION.

"What is a friend?" asks Aristotle. And then he replies, "A single soul dwelling in two bodies." The very essence of a person attempting success requires the development of relationships; friendly relationships, where possible. Don't misunderstand, not necessarily *best* friend relationships. But, keep in mind, enemies are rarely, if ever, out to help you! *Friendly* relationships, then, are a must.

So, no matter how much you consider yourself a "loner," one who *thinks* he or she doesn't need any other person to achieve your success (or, for that matter, live *any* part of your life), realize this is a disastrous misconception.

Though there are, no doubt, an exception or two, the vast majority – stress *vast* – have been successful because they have *not* gone it alone. Think about those odds for a moment.

Success is strongly linked to mentors and coaches and mastermind relationships. The friendlier the better. The evidence provided below from those who have been extremely successful cannot be ignored.

You win by establishing... a relationship and trust.

David Brock

One important word. A good relationship is always – *always* – built on trust. Break that trust and the relationship will be harmed. Sometimes irrevocably.

So, the one rule that must be stressed here is never lie. *Never.* Because if you do, you will *never* redeem yourself to the point in the relationship you were at, that moment before your lie. It will always be viewed as betrayal.

There is a corollary to this. When you make an honest mistake, have the courage to quickly admit it... and apologize. The quicker the better. You want to avoid even the appearance of betrayal. Which even mistakes can cause.

You *must* have enough personal character to refrain from lying. At the same time, be ready to quickly apologize. Trusting relationships are built on such principles.

Jessica Peterson (Chapter 2) sees the success of any undertaking, for her especially that of her business, in developing relationships.

She notes the usual questions she keeps being asked from people are, "How did you create so much success? How were you tops in sales? How are you so articulate on social media? How did you grow your word of mouth about marketing?"

Surprisingly, she admits she is not an aggressive sales person. In fact, *sales* is a word that does not really resonate with her. If someone wants to hire Jessica – great. If not, it's okay with her. She holds no ill-will.

It is her perspective that business offerings come from a place of educating people that she can help them with solutions to their problems.

Once people see she can help, it changes their mindset and they look at their current challenges from a different perspective. This in itself helps gain their trust. And in educating and bringing solutions to problems, she finds people are willing to pay for it. Further, when she has helped them, then they will suggest to others by making referrals, because they know what she has done *for them* can also help others.

The key to all of this is to sincerely take an interest in people.

Jessica has a quote that she really likes: *Your relationships are worth more than a hundred thousand dollars.* If you really believe this and live it, people will see that and a bond of trust will begin to grow.

"To begin to build that type of relationship, I just kind of step back and listen to what perspective clients have to say. Usually people that really value who you are as an individual will begin to open up to you.

"In my responding to them, they see I am so passionate and excited to help, to *want* to teach and guide them towards their own success. Sometimes all it takes is to just step back and listen. This begins to build relationships.

"And relationships are critical to personal and professional development. Good ones are priceless."

Lane Etheridge (Chapter 2), whose early teaching job led him to a desire for helping his students not only learn Algebra, but also help build their characters, advocated forming a Master Mind relationship.

The Master Mind concept, advocated by Napoleon Hill, describes a specifically designed process where at least two people work together in a spirit of harmony to attain a specific goal, a definite purpose.

Lane sees it as the *iron sharpening iron* concept. He strongly suggests you need to join yourself in that type of relationship.

He notes that the concept is grounded in the fact one idea creates more ideas: Two heads are better than one, as the cliché goes. This is especially true if the other person is experienced and working as your mentor.

That mentor then provides insights from his or her experience, thus saving you a lot of "learning by experience," which can be costly in time as well as money. By working together, Lane observes, the end result will be something that was never possible if working alone.

With that in mind, it's very important for you to be around people who are already ahead of where you currently are, in experience, technique, etc. Individuals who, though working with you, are thinking differently. It helps provide a new perspective.

Lane's own Master Mind program teaches speech presentation techniques, as well as the processes to get his clients on more stages. He also has an authorship program to help people who write.

> "Throughout our programs we teach three things – the CAR Formula. In reverse order, 'R' is *recognition*. How to become more recognizable as an expert in your field. 'A' is *authority*. How you become a more credible resource for people because the value you bring to the marketplace dictates your income. And the 'C' is *collaboration* and *contribution*. How you actually go out there and make a bigger difference in the world.

> "All of this is related to, actually hinges upon, relationships. That's what we focus on,

from our live events to our coaching to our
digital marketing to the authorship program.
Relationships."

A significant part of the issue of relationship is that of
developing one with a mentor who can guide you. Jim Vaughn
(Chapter 1) says this is critical.

He notes the number one piece of advice he gives everybody is
to find a good mentor. Find somebody out there who has been
successful, who is better at doing what you want to do. Then,
learn everything they know so you can use it to be successful
yourself.

He advises, you have to know that when you wake up in the
morning, it's your responsibility to go out and, as he views it,
kill your share of fire-breathing dragons out there. He notes
that is not always easy.

You need to find out from people who have already done this
successfully how did they do it, so that when you go out there
you know exactly what to do, and you're not lost when you
have to do it. Gain from the wisdom of others.

Jim reflects that his whole life has been based on mentors.

He stresses that the thing to be aware of is that some people
follow small-minded mentors. And then they wonder why they
fail at their achievements. Others have sought out the super
brains, those who have been tremendously successful. If you
choose this latter group, you too can become as great, if not
greater. Again, he advises, choose wisely!

"Further, every mentor I have ever embraced makes it very clear that there is *rarely* a silver bullet shortcut to success. The truth of the matter is, for these mentors, there were *no* shortcuts. They realized that if you're expecting success, *and* you are willing to do what is required to attain it, you will attract success into your life."

Bob Holmes (Chapter 5), the One-Man Volleyball Team, also sees the importance of an *unexpected* relationship. He knows that, at times, overcoming an issue or problem is resolved by people who unknowingly help.

"It's always amazing at the moment of something going wrong or something troubling me, there's always somebody there. At that moment, a person comes along who is an encouragement. It just totally amazes me how that happens. And at the time that I need it. It's just incredible.

"I've been in some instances where somebody gets mad at me, often because there's something they didn't like about what I'm doing. Or maybe what I said hit them in the wrong way.

"Right after somebody says, or does, something negative to me, someone else shows up right at that moment. The person might be someone from the audience or even the opposing team. And they let me know what I've said or done *helped them.* Often, they say how it really changed their life for the better. At that moment, when I might be downcast, they help brighten my spirits… while, at the same time, I have mentored them!"

This just shows how helpful, how critical – and at times, how *unique* – relationships actually are!

Don't attempt success without them!

9   GUIDEPOSTS

Does not wisdom call? For by wisdom kings reign;
riches and honor and enduring wealth are with her.

King Solomon

Guide-post *n.* something that directs a
person in a course of life: MARKER.

There are many who have gone before us who have achieved
success. For some it was hit-or-miss, almost blindly groping
in the darkness of a venture or field of endeavor never tried
before.

Thomas Alva Edison's 1,000 failures before he produced a
successful lightbulb comes to mind, as it is legendary. As does
Christopher Columbus and his adventure to sail west into a
hostile sea whose "flatness" would lead to his, and his crew's,
demise. The naysayers said so.

But, whether by trial-and-error or simple pre-planning, there
are many witnesses to the means which lead to success.

So, there is wisdom in harkening to those who have gone on
and become successful before us. The men and women whose

testimonies speak from this book say so. Each has one or more guideposts that have been an inspiration – and a beacon – showing them the way.

They want to share these in the hopes that, having already successfully "gone out ahead," they may lead you along that very same path to success.

To aide you, in case a particular person's insights in these pages has caught your attention and you want to search them out first, the list is alphabetical.

CHRIS CAYER suggests that one read *Conflicting Accounts: The Creation and Crash of the Saatchi & Saatchi Advertising Empire* by Kevin Goldman. However, he advises that it is probably one of the worst written books he has ever read in his life. It is not an easy read, but it is so exhaustively well researched. The data that is presented, the quotes, the interviews, the information, the industry information, is outstanding.

The author, Kevin Goldman, is a journalist. He's got the journalistic training and experience in getting the raw data and developing it into a narrative. Chris believes Goldman has done an amazing job, in part because he is obviously well trusted by the two Saatchi Brothers: Charles and Maurice, the founders of Saatchi and Saatchi. At one point theirs was the world's largest ad agency.

Chris sees this as an important book because it talks about the rise and fall of the mega advertisement agencies. It presents how the entire advertising industry has built itself up, been obliterated, built itself back up again, then been obliterated again. Goldman then reveals how these agencies reconfigured and re-tooled themselves.

Further, he shows how every business in the world interacts with them, how every consumer in the world interacts with them. Goldman's writing is not just engaging, it hooks you into understanding how advertising impacts everything you do. And how it impacts and changes society itself.

It's a remarkable book both about business, how you run your business, and its impact on your business if you are successful. You will also learn about leverage, what it is, when it goes well, and when it goes poorly… and when it gets out of hand.

It clearly demonstrates the impact of personal relationships, of managing a staff, of managing your clients, of meeting client expectations, and failing to meet those expectations. It has all those things, to include all those messy things that business people live with every day. In Chris' eyes it is an amazing book because of its context. But, again, keep in mind it was written so badly.

Chris' favorite quote: *Fight the fights that need fighting – don't just fight the fights that you can win.* It speaks for itself.

LANE ETHERIDGE has a recommendation for insights into being successful, which he does not hesitate in sharing: the Bible. He sees it as the best *business* book in the world, especially the book of Proverbs, where one can gain insight into living a successful life.

Lane's favorite quote: *Ask. Seek. Knock.* He observes that most people don't even start with the first, *Ask.* Who, What, When

Where, Why, and How need to be asked. Then, one needs to *Seek* answers to those questions. The only way to do that is to *Knock*. It is the knocking that opens doors to solutions.

STEPHANIE FRANK is an avid reader. She shared those books that had the greatest impact on her professionally and personally.

From a business perspective, she offers Michael Gerber's books, *E-Myth* and *E-Myth Enterprise*. She notes *E-myth* is all about systems and how you work on those systems in order to make your own business work well. Further, Gerber challenges the reader to create a business with a conscience; a business that is not only interested in making money, but also looks to being responsible for people in the process.

Her recommendation on a personal side is Louise Hay's book *You Can Heal Your Life*. The author provides her coaching systems through how you think and feel and behave around a difficult situation. In her case, it was a major illness.

Stephanie notes that there has been a lot of science that talks about the mind-body connection and how emotions are damaged cells in your body which cause disease. The second half of the book is very fascinating because it explains things like what pain in certain areas of your body actually means, which she finds very interesting material.

Stephanie's favorite quote reflects her own belief in leadership. It comes from Carly Fiorina, then president of Hewlett-Packard: *The leader's greatest obligation is to make possible an environment where people's minds and hearts can be inventive, brave, human, and strong. Where people can aspire to do useful and significant things. Where people can aspire to change the world.*

BOB HOLMES favorite book is obvious to all who know him: the Bible. He too sees the book of Proverbs as providing solid principles for establishing standards for one's life. Practical standards.

Bob's favorite secular quote is based on his belief that in spite of obstacles, a person should keep going forward: *Turn opposition into opportunity through the omnipotence of God.*

PAUL HOYT has done a lot of soul searching over the years. This has led him to publish a book that speaks to some of the things he's found and would like to share with others: *Remember the Spirit: A Simple and Gentle Pathway to Your Higher Self.* He adds his reason for this suggestion is not because he wrote it. It is because, for the first time he stepped out and said what he really believed and so he wants to share his journey that it might help others.

As to a favorite quote, Paul refers to one of his own poems. He shares it to guide others to their own success: *It's not about me or the things that I do. I just get out of the way and let spirit come through... As it has been for me so it can be for you, Just step to one side and let spirit come through.*

ERIC LOFHOLM wants to share a favorite book. He acknowledges it is little-known: *Future Diary* by Mark Victor Hansen. It's such a simple goal setting book, and a very easy read. Mark is one of the authors behind *Chicken Soup for the Soul.*

Eric, who is a big quote guy, has as his much-loved quote from Tony Robbins: *The past does not equal the future.* Eric sees this saying that the future is a clean slate. Every person has got the opportunity for new beginnings and new opportunity, even if he or she struggled in an area of their life in the past.

KEN MACARTHUR offers two suggestions for books that he sees as having a positive impact on guiding one to success. The first is Jack Canfield's *Success Principles*. He also sees books by Seth Godin such as *Tipping Point* or *Black Swan* or *What The Dog Saw* or *Good To Great* as being really powerful reads. He also recommends biographies, especially of the U.S. presidents, because their decisions had significant, often serious, impact on a great many people.

Dr. JEFF MAGEE recommends a number of books, especially the classic success books by such authors as Napoleon Hill and W. Clement Stone. Hill's *Think and Grow Rich*, he feels, is a great book, and goes on to note it has been around forever. As has *Success Through Positive Attitude*. Then there is Dale Carnegie's *How to Win Friends and Influence People*. Last, he suggests the book by Stephen Covey – *Seven Habits of Highly Effective People* which, he observes with a smile, when you look at the seven habits, you've got to laugh because they're so obvious.

Dr. Jeff also believes you should read what *you* write. He believes it is not egotistical; it's listening to the voice in your head, especially when it has led to your own success. Two of his books, *Fist Factor*™ and *The Player Capability Index Model*™ are on his list.

Dr. WILL MORELAND has a unique book suggestion for those interested in success. It is for him *the* anchor foundation book. It has a funny title, but don't let that throw you off. The name of the book is *Why Should White Guys Have All The Fun?* It was written by a gentleman named Reginald F. Louis who was a lawyer raised in Baltimore, Maryland's inner-city. He was an African-American who used his brain and his business savvy to be the first African-American man to buy a billion – with a 'B' – dollar company. He bought Beatrice International.

While he was working as a lawyer, he dealt with a number of leveraged, buy-out companies. One day he realized he could do this on his own; go out and buy companies. And have as much fun as the guys he was working for were having. That's the inside joke to the book's title: *Why Should White Guys Have All The Fun?* Again, don't let the title fool you, the book, Dr. Will observes, has so much practical application.

Dr. Will offers a final reflection, his favorite quote. It is one of his own and he offers it because it speaks directly from his heart. It addresses the issue that time is the great equalizer: *We are all equal in time, but we are separated by what we do with that time.* Use that time wisely!

From the close relationship JESSICA PETERSON has had with her grandmother, she quickly identifies her "go to" book. For the third time here in the Guideposts, we see it is the book of Proverbs. Jessica also stresses that the wisdom contained in this book of the Bible is not just wisdom, it is *practical* wisdom. And because of that, Jessica observes, it can be applied anywhere. Nor is it limited to any race, nationality, religious or even political beliefs. It is a manual to live a fruitful, simple, and successful life.

Jessica has three quotes that have guided her towards her success. First, *Keep It Simple.* She feels we over-complicate things. Second is one of her own: *A New Experience Is The Best Experience.* The third is linked to her business: *Who Will You WOW Today?* Who is the one person that can be impacted today for his or her good?

KEN ROCHON has some solid book recommendations. He too suggests *E-myth* by Michael Gerber. There is also *The Go-Giver* by Bob Burg. The theme of Burg's book is about not what you get from life, but what you give to life! It's about what you give to networking opportunities and what you give to relationships, especially how to start them. He also agrees with Dr. Jeff Magee that if you've written an outstanding book, there is no reason why you can't cite your own writings as a favorite

Ken has a favorite quote… and he acknowledges it is a bit raw. It is from Sir Richard Branson, the British business magnate who founded the Virgin Group, which includes Virgin Atlantic Airline: *I'd rather have a hole in my company than an ass-hole.*

Ken observes that if you apply that to your business, or any venture for that matter, you will make it a point to keep a jerk out of your company. You certainly won't let someone negative into it. You won't let anyone in your business who is not complimentary with your ideology and your team needs. You know the adage: One bad apple spoils the whole bunch. For Ken, Branson's quote makes this very clear.

CHRIS SALEM identifies his favorite book as *The Power of Focus* by Jack Canfield, Mark Victor Hansen and Les Hewitt. Though not one of their more famous books, it still is really packed with everything that you want to know about personal development. Further, it relates to not only your personal life, but also to your business. It demonstrates how you can really transform yourself in both of these two areas. Chris believes you'll get a lot of great nuggets, and shifts in mindset, from reading it.

As to a favorite quote, Chris quickly identifies one. It is from Jack Canfield: *Everything is on the other side of fear.* Because a lot of people live on this side of fear, they literally live within that fear. It holds them back from so many things that they could do within their lifetime.

Chris sees this as a crime because the strengths and the abilities that they have, they could offer value to others with. Yet, they are stagnant because they live in, and are trapped in, fear. But, when you're able to come out of your comfort zone and go beyond it, everything you desire and everything that you could offer, that can help others, is on that other side.

Dr. LEN SCHWARTZ suggests a book by his former partner, who has since passed away, entitled *The Ultimate Sales Machine.* It is an excellent book that provides invaluable clarity and direction as it pertains to lead generation and sales. For Dr. Len, it is probably the best book on those topics.

As to a favorite quote, Dr. Len chooses one from Jim Rohn: *If it's important to you, you'll find a way. If it's not, you'll find an excuse.* Like it or not, he observes, that quote will get you to realize the truth every single day: Are you doing whatever it takes?

Next to the Bible, which also contains innumerable of his favorite quotes, Coach ANDRE M. "A.M." WILLIAMS offers another book as a guide to success, which he has used to guide him to his own success. He highly recommends *The Secret to Selling Anything* by Harry Brown. Coach A.M. suggests one read it with the intention of applying it to their life. He goes on to caution that you don't want to end up like some individuals who jumped into personal development and have a billion-dollar library, but less than a hundred dollars-worth of application.

As to his *favorite* Bible quote, he identifies a verse from Galatians, chapter four: *Now I say, that an heir as long as he is as a child, differs nothing from a slave though he be lord of all.*

Coach A.M. sees this as being so huge because it speaks to the issue of maturity. Paul the Apostle, who wrote this, is basically saying that despite the fact that even an heir – someone who is going to receive a huge inheritance – as long as that person is as a child, he or she is no different than a lowly slave. Why? Because they lack the maturity to make wise decisions. Just like a slave, who has *no* authority to make any decisions at all.

This speaks clearly to the need for an individual to mature and gain life's experiences in order to make wise decisions. Coach A.M. advises, you have to develop or you do not differ from a slave.

Powerful stuff! he observes.

10 LEADERSHIP

Leadership is influence.

John C. Maxwell

Lead-er-ship n. to go out in front and influence someone to follow: GUIDANCE.

There is a graphic making the rounds on the Internet these days that depicts a long line of wolves traveling in the wilderness. The commentary points out that the three in front are the oldest who, we are told, "set the pace." If put at the rear because they are moving so slowly, they would inevitably get left behind.

The wolves in front are followed by a set of wolves described as "the strongest." They are positioned there in order to respond to any threats encountered by the three in front "walking point." Behind these "strongest" follow the rest of the pack.

At the very rear, slightly separated from the pack, is a lone wolf. He is identified as the "leader." The commentary states his position is best to keep an eye on the whole pack and thus *lead* them.

The point that is ultimately stressed is that the old concept of leadership, that of "being in front," is not only outdated, but entirely wrong. True leadership, they say, is from the rear.

We are going to show that this "new concept" is definitely wrong. And probably why organizations can be run-into-the-ground and thus fail, should they be following it.

Management is efficiency
in climbing the ladder of success;
leadership determines whether the ladder
is leaning against the right wall....

Stephen Covey

Let's stay with the wolf motif for a moment. At a crossroad intersection, should the three old wolves up front decide to go to the left – and step out in that direction – but the "leader" at the rear wants to go right, how can he effect that change in direction of the pack? *He must go to the front* and redirect those wolves there to guide the pack in the correct direction.

Leadership is *always* from the front. The lone wolf keeping an eye on the activities in the rear is *managing*. It is the three wolves up front, especially the one at the very front, who is leading, setting the direction that the others will follow.

Just ask Dr. Will Moreland (Chapter 3), who learned this valuable lesson while in the U.S. Army.

"I did my basic training at Fort Knox, Kentucky, my advanced at Aberdeen Proving Grounds, Maryland. Then I got stationed in Germany. For the first time in my life I was thousands of miles away from home. I was in an environment I never experienced before. An environment that could literally change my life.

"In Germany I found a mentor. He was a Sergeant Major, the highest-ranking non-commissioned officer (NCO), on our base.

"He began to mentor and show me the results that structure and discipline bring. By structure and discipline, I mean such things as being on time. Completing every job to a military standard. Obeying those in authority over you. All character traits that lead to success – and which others want to follow.

"He guided me to learn what true leadership was. That is, in the sense of actually going out 'in-front' to demonstrate what was to be accomplished, and then instilling in me, and others, the willingness to do the same."

A leader "goes out in front" and demonstrates how it is done. And then he or she motivates others to follow. Leaders set the course by being "out front." *There is no other way to lead.*

That is why Webster's Dictionary defines it as such: To direct on a course or in a direction… especially by going in advance. In contrast to "going out in front," *managers* see that the direction chosen is actually followed; they see it "gets done."

With this as background, let's look at the aspects of leadership.

Leadership is the combination of two things:
It is competence and character.

General H. Norman Schwartzkopf

Effective leadership consists of two main requirements. We have seen these consistently in each of the successful individuals who have spoken in this book.

The first is *competency*. This is decision-making ability coupled with one's aptitude and skills to attain success of an undertaking. And, don't confuse enthusiasm with competency. Because someone says he or she *wants* to achieve a goal, doesn't mean they have the necessary ability to actually accomplish that.

There are two elements of competency. First, one must be *efficient*. Efficiency is doing the thing right. As an example, if one is painting the exterior second floor of a house and is working off of a trapeze line rather than a stable ladder, the house may be getting painted (completing the task), but it is not the best (or safest) way to accomplish that goal. People will not follow if they sense things are being done the *wrong way*.

The second element is being *effective*. Effectiveness is doing the right thing. As an example, firefighters may demonstrate efficient skills in deploying their men and equipment to fight a fire. But if they do so on the wrong house, one that is not on fire, all that skill is wasted (and the house on fire may burn to the ground). People will not follow if they sense they are doing the *wrong thing*.

There are two ways competency may be gained. The first is through *good training*. Tried-and-true efficient and effective methods are best passed down from others with applicable experience. Learning from those who have "gone before" reduces, possibly eliminates, the hit-or-miss methods that often lead to unnecessary failures.

Coupled with good training is *acceptable experience*, experience *you* have gained. By acceptable, we mean previous successes and failures, *if* learning takes place from those experiences. Too often an event occurs and there is no follow-up analysis to determine what went well and what did not. It's an experience, yes, but what has been learned to apply later towards future success if it isn't analyzed and "learning" gained?

The second requirement of effective leadership is *character*. This is the internal, intrinsic value system that is consistently applied in external actions. These values demonstrate traits that are conducive to decision-making capability and from which others are, thus, willing to follow you.

These traits are demonstrated in three ways. First, there is the conviction to "get the job done." This includes, as we have seen, the willingness to "get the job started." Leaders set the direction by being the first to step out and set the direction and pace.

A second way character is demonstrated is shown in one's courage to persevere. This is usually seen in a person's selflessness as he or she sacrifices to achieve their goal.

The third demonstration of character is a willingness to accept responsibility. By being accountable, one is seen as reliable, the

"I've got your back" attitude that draws people to follow you. Whiners and buck-passers need not apply!

Having identified what leadership is, it is now important to define the three main responsibilities of *effective* leadership.

First of all, a leader must properly *define the current reality.* Wishful thinking will not make you an effective leader. Willingness to face harsh realities will. If you don't know where you are really at, how can you chart the correct course?

Which leads to the second aspect of effective leadership. A leader must *provide a vision of the future.* He or she must be a visionary. How else can a "direction" be ascertained? The age-old saying holds true, "If you don't know where you are going, you'll never get there!"

Lastly, a leader must *establish procedures,* which include motivating others to accomplish the goals being set. These procedures will bridge the present reality with the future's vision by creating the steps necessary to realize that vision.

The reader will quickly notice that all three of these elements for effective leadership require a person who is competent and who possesses a solid character.

As part of establishing procedures to bridge the present with the future, a leader must be not only a visionary, seeing where he or she wants to go, but also must be a living symbol of how to get there.

The vernacular of today is "walk the talk." This must be done in a highly visible way so that trust is developed causing others to be willing to follow. Part of "walking the talk" includes being a buck-stopper, that character trait of being responsible.

The last aspect of establishing procedures is that of team-building. A leader needs to put the right people in the right place and at the right time. As Ken Rochon noted

> "I don't know all the answers. So, I'm attracting people to be on my team that can help me with those answers. *That's* a mindset that excites me!"

And it should excite the team as well. Because a team is an *enthusiastic* set of competent people, each having a clearly defined, individual role. At the same time, they are associated together working in a common activity towards a common goal. And they are working together cohesively in a trusting relationship as they exercise personal discipline, making individual sacrifices where necessary, for the good of the team.

People who work together will win,
whether it be against complex football defenses,
or the problems of modern society.

Vince Lombardi

As a leader, one must see that the team has a common purpose. This includes a shared understanding of what must be done, the philosophy and values that should guide decision-making, and a belief that everyone on the team has a part to play in its success.

The team must also have common knowledge. This includes a high level of individual job knowledge, an understanding how the overall organization operates, and how an individual's contribution fits into the overall process.

Finally, the team must have common sense. Individual members must use practical attitudes to get things done, know they are entitled to act on one's own initiative (within reason), and have the moral authority to solve problems rather than slavishly go "by the book."

In closing, there is one aspect of leadership that should be considered by all. It is the concept of servant-leader. Instead of the classic design of an organization, that of the pyramid with the leader at the top being supported by the other levels below, the servant-leader's pyramid is inverted. In this model, the servant-leader supports the activities of the organization... even, and especially, as he or she leads it.

The supreme quality of leadership is integrity.

Dwight Eisenhower

A FINAL WORD

A man cannot be comfortable without his own approval.

Mark Twain

In-ner Peace *n.* the state of being content
with our self: SELF-HARMONY.

This book began with a look at elements of Max Ehrman's poem *Desiderata*. In part, it noted "you have a right to be here."

Building off of that observation, we proposed you not only have a right to be here, but your very presence indicates there is a Divine Calling and Purpose for you as well! Hopefully, through these pages you have been guided to discovering *your* purpose. And, from your reading, you should now have the tools necessary to begin to pursue that purpose... and make it work!

Your pursuit of making it work rests upon you seeing your effort as heroic. Yes, heroic! If you understand that your work has eternal significance as it impacts not only your generation, but, possibly, generations to follow, you can awaken your heart and mind to pursue your dream regardless of whatever circumstances you find yourself.

This can happen when you define your goal as a cause: The good or service you will ultimately produce as an extension of your very being. And, when geared to serve others in a need that you have identified, it will have a positive effect. A heroic effect.

This is because it is infused with your highest ideals – a cause that speaks to your heart and makes you speak passionately about what you do. Imagine sharing and engaging in a cause that calls forth courage and perseverance, demands passionate focus, fosters a revolutionary spirit in order to achieve the near-impossible… and gives people hope for a better world.

So, we ask, Is there some indignity out there that is calling you to fix? What impossible dream has your name on it? And, what if your "work" becomes your "calling?" Once you identify that, you have clearly seen your purpose. We think this is a Divine Purpose.

That is why others may not see the need you see. That is why they see no purpose in addressing it. But you do. You see it as a consequential, awe-inspiring problem that *you* are trying to solve. It is your goal; your adventure to reach it. If you don't take on this goal, who else would do it? There is a cause out there with your name on it. Something you care about deeply, even if others don't.

That is why, *for you* it is heroic! When your goal becomes a cause, what follows is a movement.

Just ask Bob Salomon.

For two-and-a-half decades Bob worked as a corrections officer for the state of New Jersey. New Jersey, it brings to mind *mafia*, among other types of criminals. Bob pretty much saw it all.

> "Regardless of the reason the person was in prison, I would often hear a consistent lament: 'If only I hadn't made that first bad decision.' Consistently, whether in jail for the first time or as a result of a lifetime of crime, the inmate would relate how an initial bad decision led to the next. They eventually reached a point where they couldn't get out of the web they had weaved.
>
> "That first bad decision was all it took. Many an inmate wished they could undo it."

Bob saw a need. And he had a desire to meet it… head-on.

> "Working in corrections helped me lay down a foundation to start understanding how the positive was needed. An intervention was needed. If I could reach kids well before a decision point, when they were young enough to understand, but before they acted on a bad decision, I knew I could help them.
>
> "And what young kid doesn't like some kind of sport? I just saw that if I could use sports as a way to get their attention, they might listen to my message."

It was not too longer after this that Bob met Debbie Moldovan, Keri Conkling, and Lisa Funari-Willever, the authors of the book *A Glove Of Their Own*.

Glove tells the story of underprivileged kids who inspire an adult to share in their experience of playing sandlot baseball with little or no equipment. The "old man" goes on to help them by donating the equipment necessary for them to more fully play, and thus enjoy, the game.

For many, the book's story brings the adult reader back to his or her own childhood, and is written to tug at the heart strings. The theme of the story is the concept of "paying it forward." A person pays it forward when, with a simple act of kindness, they unselfishly help others, not expecting anything in return. In *Glove*'s case, the message is clear: Helping youth.

For Bob, the book became a personal project as he heartily began to promote it. To that end, he used *Glove* as a fund-raiser for kids employing the great game of baseball as a springboard. His efforts eventually picked up support from such well-known sports companies as Rawlings, Louisville Slugger, and Modell's.

From there, it gained the support of non-profit organizations such as Covenant House, Mattingly Charities, The Yogi Berra Museum & Learning Center, and Joe Torre's Safe at Home Foundation. The greatest endorsements come from major league athletes including Tommy John, Don Mattingly, Mike Sweeney, Jason Grilli, Eric Chavez, Nelson Cruz, Bud Harrelson, Michael Cuddyer, Roy White, Phil Niekro, Jim Eisenreich, Shea Hillenbrand, and many more. He would develop a friendship with Doug Glanvile, former major league baseball player and, at the time, an analyst with the ESPN network.

These athletes embraced Bob's perspective that they, the role models to the next generation, could positively invest in the lives of our youth and the local communities in which they reside and play.

> "When you get the support of professional athletes, those who really appreciate the opportunities of playing the game on a professional level and who realize that the blessings they receive for that accomplishment are just that, blessings, then you can accomplish significant benefits for children.

> "Instead of just talking about it, these professionals are doing something. They realize kids are our future, and professional athletes are often the role models who can help shape their lives. So, in bringing these athletes together to coordinate their efforts to pay it forward to children—their biggest fans—much can be accomplished.

> "And the athletes themselves are excited to do this. They see it as a way to promote a positive message and change things that are detrimental to these children.

> "It also helps develop a positive image for the world of sports itself. Which, these days, it could use."

With his success in promoting *Glove* as a confirmation that this was not only a passion for Bob, but actually his calling, he began to work on his own book. That effort would produce *Beyond The Laces*.

Beyond The Laces has as its storyline the circumstances which surround a sick child whose parents desire for him to be well. That healing is dependent on the child's own will to be healed. The reader sees early on this child's love of the game of football, and his deep adoration of a professional player identified only by his jersey, *number 87*.

With the desperation of his parents for their son's well-being, the father takes a leap of faith. He reaches out to player 87 hoping this high-profile athlete has enough heart for a fan, the boy, and his parents, all of them in a serious need of hope.

> "The story began to take real shape a year before I retired. The writing in itself would take enormous effort to actually draft, edit, and polish. It was especially challenging because I wanted to stay with the form of poetry that had been so successful in *Glove*. The writing alone was eight months of solid, focused effort.

> "But it wasn't just the writing. I wanted every other page to be a full-page, colored drawing of what the text was stating. Finding an artist proved equally as difficult. There are plenty of them out there, but I wanted someone who felt – had equal enthusiasm for – this project as I did.

"Ken Jones, a professional artist who has done a number of sports illustrations well before *Beyond The Laces* was-even-a-thought, actually took me over a year to finally stumble across. I had been looking far and wide – *nationwide* is a better description – until I met Ken. The first time we sat down together I knew I had found my artist. The rest, as they say, is history.

"And the result? Ken's drawings for the book are spectacular!"

Then, of course, there was finding a publisher.

"I had so many doors slammed in my face. Add to that the 'We'll get back to you; don't call us, we'll call you.' I was virtually on my last phone call when I reached out to Charley Ambrogio at CMYK Printing. He listened patiently. A couple of questions later we set up a face-to-face meeting.

"From that phone call, not only would a publisher be found, but a friendship would eventually develop. And Charley has become a valuable member of the BTL team. When I do a school presentation, Charley comes along and answers any questions dealing with the publishing end of things. I mean, how many publishers do that?!"

With the inspirational message of *Beyond The Laces*, a number of professional football personalities have endorsed Bob's work. Coach Herm Edwards, and players like Roger Staubach, Mark Brunnell, Victor Green, Bill Bates, amongst others.

> "We have the support of these known sports personalities because *Beyond the Laces* is football at its best; a narrative of how one of America's greatest past times is the backdrop to a story that provides inspiration to overcome great adversity.
>
> "The book has been written to inspire not only children, but adults as well. And many of these athletes have noted it is especially powerful as parents read it aloud to their children.
>
> "But, the real goal of this football book is to make all athletes come together to help kids. We want to tour throughout hospitals, and other places where the needs exist, going around the country with various sports figures to send the message about not giving up. My dream is that professional sports will use the book to help promote this message and that the athletes themselves will be given the opportunity for a positive impact on children and just show that people do care."

It is safe to say Bob Solomon's heartfelt story has spawned an unstoppable movement through his charitable heart and an unmatched passion to help children. He has already been involved in such projects as visiting a children's ward with the Belief Project's Christmas in July program to bring joy to kids in the hospital, Covenant House activities helping homeless youth, and speaking engagements at schools where the *Beyond The Laces* themes of kindness and respect are used to reinforce education's anti-bullying campaigns.

Bob is using sports to help those in need. As Dough Glanville, former major league baseball player and ESPN sports analyst noted, "This amazing story and movement is a runaway train, and it will one day bring the humanity back to all of the sports we hold dear by employing our greatest resource: People."

Bob Salomon, former corrections officer, has found, and is using, his passion to serve and help others. In a second career, he has identified his Divine Calling and Purpose. And has had the courage to pursue it!

> Perhaps we shall learn,
> as we pass through this age,
> that the "other self"
> is more powerful than the physical self
> we see when we look into a mirror.

Napoleon Hill

Epilogue

Success is not a sprint... it is a marathon.
Look, then, not just to any particular moment,
but rather to one's entire lifetime.

Ben Gay III

Ben Gay III is rightly considered the Senior Statesman of Success. He embodies, at a high level of exceptional excellence, all of the character traits defined in these pages.

Thus, with him having begun our book, it is fitting that he end it. You will see in his interview, set here in its entirety, all of the aspects raised in this writing, which lead to success. In this case, his, Ben's, success... throughout his life!

Ben Gay III has been called a living legend in the world of sales. After 50 years in professional selling, he has been the #1 salesperson in every organization in which he has worked. There is no greater source for insight into what sales success really is than Ben Gay III.

Ben has worked continuously as a 100% commissioned salesperson since he was 14 years old. Sixty years of unbroken commissioned selling! That is why he is one of the most famous, popular, and powerful sales trainers in the world.

With that experience, Ben currently writes, publishes, and produces "The Closers," a series of books, audios, videos, newsletters, tele-trainings, and live seminars that are considered to be "The Foundation of Professional Selling." And his two newsletters, "The Closer Update" and "The Closer Alert" have been called "the voices of professional selling."

Further, the book he did for J. Douglas Edwards, "Sales Closing Power!" (one of 24 books he has written or ghost-written) is considered required reading for those who call themselves professional salespeople. One can easily see why Ben was the founder and is the current Executive Director of The National Association of Professional Salespeople (NAPS).

This incredible salesman has shared his knowledge with literally millions around the world who are in sales through his resource materials and 5,000+ live speeches or seminars. Added to this, Ben has done countless television and radio appearances.

Yet, Ben's achievements are not limited to sales. He was also nicknamed "Attitude Coach" for the National Air and Space Administration's (NASA) astronauts and ground crews of Apollo 15, 16, and 17, having been chosen by none other than Colonel James Irwin, Commander Apollo 15.

Additionally, in 1976 Ben launched the 800-number call center industry by founding The National Communications

Center. Taken for granted today, this innovative model started a business revolution that changed the way we all shop and communicate.

This highly successful businessman and his lovely wife Gigi live near Lake Tahoe in the little Northern California town of Placerville, California – where the California Gold Rush began!

For all of his accomplishments, and as with many success stories, Ben's beginnings were less then auspicious. For that reason, his story should provide hope to those who may themselves be struggling to persevere.

He was a straight-A student until 5th grade. Then, he admits, "Puberty, or something, kicked in – I don't know what happened to me in the fifth grade. I turned into the class clown; the proverbial smart aleck. And my grades fell."

As his academics slid, so did his deportment. Eventually, in high school, he was thrown out of public school.

Fortunately, as Ben says, "My father and mother had some money … so I was sent to a private school. Had they not had money, I would have been sent to a reform school."

But, his conduct did not improve much. In fact, many of his classmates, some delinquents themselves, were just as rebellious, if not more so. In about two years he was thrown out of the private prep school as well!

Ben returned home to Atlanta and, one would think *miraculously*, was accepted back into his former public high school. But, things had changed for him. "In my senior year, I became a normal human being. The private school experience had done some good for me. It straightened me up."

There was another factor for Ben's change of attitude: He found a mentor in school; actually *two* mentors.

The first would be Ms. Griffin, the Senior English class teacher. On his first day back at school, Ben mistakenly went to the wrong classroom. Once redirected, he hurried to the correct one… but he was late!

> "Now I'm late for class on the first day returning from reform school. I come skidding into the room – literally. It was like that Kramer guy on "Seinfeld" skidding through the door.
>
> "Ms. Griffin looked up from her desk, and we didn't know each other, but because I was late and because everybody laughed when I came skidding into the room, she said, 'Mr. Gay, I presume.' I remember thinking, 'Uh oh. This is not good!' So, she got up and got one of the student desks, brought it up, spun it around, and put it next to her desk – facing the class.
>
> "She then said, 'I've been waiting for you. I know some of the teachers who have worked with you in the past and I know a lot about you – good and bad. But, you're going to sit here right next to me this year and, no matter

what your past has been, you are going to win
the state writing championship. *And* you're
going to speak at graduation.'

"I thought, first – that was sort of a scary
burden to put on me since I could barely write
my own name; and second – I thought if you
spoke at graduation, you were the Valedictorian
or Salutatorian. So I thought to myself, 'You
have no idea who you are messing with, because
there's not even a remote chance of me speaking
at graduation!' "

Through the mentoring of Ms. Griffin, a teacher who finally
understood him and what he deeply needed, Ben actually did
go on to win the state writing championship! And that June, at
his class' graduation exercise, he walked in front of over 3,000
people… and gave the opening prayer, which Ms. Griffin had
helped Ben craft and memorize. Such is the impact a patient
mentor can have on even the rowdiest of us.

Ben learned another vital lesson at graduation.

"I walked to the front of Atlanta's Municipal
Auditorium, gave the two-armed signal for
everyone to rise, and 3,000 people stood up!
I remember thinking, 'Whoa! I never had
that happen before!' And, you know, once
3,000 people stand up, pay attention while
I talk to them, and nobody shoots me, or I
don't faint or throw up, I thought . . . '*this* is
pretty neat!' "

Ben Gay III, the orator, had been born! Although it would take some years to polish his style, he would spend the rest of his adult life fulfilling what Ms. Griffin had born in him.

Then, as if one mentor were not enough, in that same senior year, Ben also had the good fortune to have Mr. Evans as his History teacher. Mr. Evans could take history and make it come alive for Ben! Instead of the dull memorization of names, dates, and places, this History teacher would cause his class to question *why* an event occurred; *what* was its underlying cause.

For Ben, it was no longer that there was an American Civil War or a World War II, but *why* they happened. And it was no longer *who* won, but *how* they won. History came alive! And so did Ben's introduction to systematic analysis: "When I get into a business situation, I can just go back in my head, thanks to Mr. Evans, and figure out how it's going to work out – because it always has throughout history!"

Though he was mentored in his senior year of high school, college turned out to be a bust.

Ben was actually elected president of the freshman class at Georgia State University. Unfortunately for him, the inauguration was three weeks after school started. Before the inauguration date rolled around, he had already dropped out. He lasted at Georgia State University three weeks!

In part, and to understand why, flashback four years:

At 14, without today's Internet or cell phones, Ben's father saw him sitting around the house just staring at the television.

Ben's dad suggested he do something to keep himself busy . . . and maybe even make some money.

"What am I going to do?" Ben asked, "I'm 14 years old." His dad said, "Well, you *could* mow lawns." "But I can't afford a lawnmower." "Well, we have one in the basement. You may not be aware of that since you've rarely used it."

So, Ben went out to knock on doors and mow lawns. He and his family lived in Atlanta, Georgia, and this was in the summer. Temperatures easily hit the high 90s or low 100s. And the humidity was almost always 90%, or more. It was like living in a steam bath, but Ben was *working* in it.

He mowed a few yards and made, in his estimation, a reasonable amount. His father then gave him some business advice – "Don't give them a price up front. Tell them to pay you what they think the job is worth when you're through, and then do a really good job." Ben agreed to give it a try.

His father's advice, literally, paid off. "Let's say I expected to come back with five dollars for a yard. I did a really good job and came back with ten or fifteen dollars – sometimes more! I said, this is pretty good.'"

Ben's only problem? He still didn't really want to do manual labor in the South . . . in the summertime. Being a lawnmower operator was just not a job he wanted to turn into a career!

His father offered Ben a second business insight:

> "Here's what you do now. You go out, get
> a few friends who are willing to work for

you, and you book the jobs. You put each of
your willing friends on a project, which you
go back and inspect. You have them do any
corrections you think are necessary, then you
collect the money. Whatever you collect, you
split with the kids 50/50."

Ben felt bad in two ways. First, he was sorry that he was only
making half the money. And he also felt bad that he wasn't
actually doing any of the work! But he got over both concerns!

His father counseled a third time. "Ben, selling *is* work. It's
the most important thing that goes on in our economy. It is
honorable to sell the jobs, inspect the jobs, collect the money,
and pay people who might otherwise not have any income."

With that insight, and encouragement, Ben began to really
sell. His income, his *half,* increased to many times what he had
made before (while working by himself). Before the summer
was over, and several summers thereafter, he had between 20
and 25 kids working for him part-time!

At his "entry level" sales venture, Ben was making more money
in the summers than several of the neighborhood's adult men.
That says a lot, as the income bracket of his neighborhood
could be judged by Atlanta's famous East Lake Country Club
(where his family belonged) being two blocks down from his
family's front door. And all of this profit on only 4½ months
of work!

Ben reflects back on this and definitely feels blessed in that
he was born into a family where everyone – including aunts

and uncles – *everyone*, either owned their own business or were partnered with someone who did.

And, of course, he was in Atlanta.

> "I grew up sitting around the dining room, the men's grill, and so on, at East Lake Country Club with my father, listening intently to the CEO's of some of the largest, most successful companies in the world. I eventually met just about all the CEO's of all the top companies in America that had Atlanta offices. You know, Home Depot is based there; Coca Cola is based there, and so many others.

> "Just about everyone I knew, through all of my role models, owned or ran their own businesses. So, I was sort of set on the path. An old friend of mine, the late great Jim Newman of PACE Seminars, coined the phrase, "Comfort Zone." My comfort zone was set high, principally by the way I was raised, and also by the people with whom I was able to associate. Those experiences and expectations didn't leave a whole lot of room for being an hourly worker somewhere."

One can see why college would not appeal to a young, energetic, *focused* Ben Gay! All of this led to Ben's start-up of his first "adult" business.

Holiday Magic Cosmetics was a multi-level marketing (MLM) company, much like the well-known Amway is today. Ben started as a distributor in the company with Jimmy Rucker (in Ben's opinion "the greatest salesperson" he ever worked with), and another friend, Cliff Beakes. They would work the business as 3-way partners.

> "We were debating who got to be president, who got to be vice president, and so on. Jimmy mumbled to me quietly, 'Be secretary and treasurer and you have the checkbook.' 'I should be president!' I snorted back. 'Secretary-treasurer gets the checkbook,' he reiterated with that knowing look in his eye. So I did it and became the treasurer. And I have to say it cut out a lot of future squabbles as I was the only one who could sign the checks!"

At Holiday Magic Cosmetics (HMC), Ben would learn his first professional-level sales lessons… the hard way.

Entry into the basic "Organizer" sales level required an entry fee of $91.42. Jimmy Rucker paid it because he was the only one who had gotten paid that week. Then the trio found out they needed to have $2,500 more to get into a better position; to *really* make money they needed to be a "Master Distributor." They raised the money and became a Master Distributor.

Then their sponsor told them they really need to be a General Distributor (another $2,500!). At that level they would make the *real money*. So, the partnership was $5,091.42 deep (in 1965 dollars) into the Holiday Magic Cosmetics program and hadn't made a dime. And they wouldn't make a dime for the next six months they were in business. Here is where Ben would learn his first professional-level sales lesson, as noted, the hard way. The jokester, Ben Gay III, had not taken professional selling seriously.

Holiday Magic Cosmetics conducted sales meetings in which prospective Distributors, like Ben and his two partners had been, would be encouraged to invest in their own HMC business.

> "One night I walked into the meeting and was met by my sponsor, Bill Dempsey. Keep in mind that our $5,091.42 was a considerable amount of money. You adjust it for inflation; $5,000 in 1965 was equivalent to about $50,000 in today's money (2017). So, it wasn't a small commitment.

> "So I walk into the meeting at the Georgian Terrace Hotel in downtown Atlanta and Bill Dempsey greets me. He says, 'Ben, how are you? I need to talk to you for a minute.' I went over and he said, 'I don't want you coming to the meetings any more.' I was shocked. He said again, 'I don't want you coming.' 'Why?' I asked. Bill looked at me seriously and said, 'You never bring anybody to the meetings. It's because you won't learn the script about how to invite someone to come.'

> "I stood there silent. 'And when the meeting is over,' he continued, 'and the people are

starting to close their prospects, because you're around all the time, new people raise their hands and ask if you would help them do that. They don't know any better. They don't know that, when you come over, you don't know the scripts on how to close the deal either.

"'And, just as bad, you can't talk at the front of the room. So, you're no help to me in the first hour of the meeting. You don't know what to say, because you won't learn *that* script either. Frankly, you're beginning to depress people. When you come in, it's like a wet blanket, so I just don't want you coming to the meetings anymore.'

"I said, 'Bill, my two partners and I have over $5,000 invested in this business, plus $50 a month to belong to the local council.' (The council was like a co-op that rented the meeting room, etc.). 'I can't *not* come to the meetings!' He said, 'Well, I will have police escort you from the meeting if you try.'"

Ben would have to learn from that self-imposed setback: He would take the profession of sales seriously from then on. He immediately went to work on memorizing the HMC sales procedures, "the scripts."

After demonstrating his ability to conduct himself in a professional manner by learning the scripts, Bill Dempsey allowed Ben back into the meetings. At the first one, Ben and Jimmy Rucker would sell over $12,000 in Distributorships.

> "I went from the first six months of that business when we made nothing, to the next six months, where we made $110,000. While holding down our full-time jobs. That money, $110,000 in 1965 dollars, is roughly a million dollars today – working part time."

Once Ben started taking sales seriously, learning the scripts, getting up early every morning and working late into the night, using the opportunity at HMC meetings, he began to make a tremendous amount of money.

A year and a half later, he moved to California. Shortly thereafter, he became president of Holiday Magic Cosmetics, which by then was the largest multi-level direct marketing company in the world.

Ben began to help grow the company. HMC now had subsidiary companies. They used the same marketing plan, but with different products. There were five different companies each in 25 different countries. In his mid-to-late twenties, Ben was running and supervising 125 companies around the world. And this with only a high school education. All because he had finally gotten *serious* about professional sales!

Through his initial ordeal at HMC, Ben had also come to understand that people are motivated basically by hope of reward or fear of loss. Yes, he knew that he had entered into business primarily because he wanted to make more money.

Yet, a fear of loss was also a human factor with which he had to contend.

He knew he could simply not let down his two buddies and lose their $5,000, especially at the outset of his business career. He wouldn't like that even now, but at that time, it wasn't even an option. With his back against the wall, it was swim or sink. From deep within his own character, he rose to the occasion and took on the responsibility that would cause him to be successful then . . . and successful throughout his business career.

It was that steadfast character that would also carry him through a primary psychological obstacle in business: the Naysayers.

Ben had made it clear that he intended to be a millionaire by the time he was 30. He was often met by the derisive, "Yeah, right." There is one particular naysaying event that he vividly remembers.

> "I was at a Thanksgiving dinner in 1966 and there was a group of families that gathered together every Thanksgiving. We did that for many, many years until the previous generation all died off. I was sitting between Aleen Harris, the next door neighbor where I was growing up, and my mother, Frances "Fran" Gay. I was making at the time about $40,000 *a month* and again, that's about $400,000 in today's 2017 dollars.

"Aleen leaned across my plate like I wasn't there; probably because I had been the little boy from next door. I guess she didn't figure she had to treat me with any dignity. She leaned across my plate and said to my mother, 'Frances, when's Ben going to get a job?'

"I was making – I know what her son was making at Gulf Oil – he was making about half-per-year of what I was making *a month*. He was at $20,000 per year and I was $40,000 a month. But, it wasn't a job with a weekly paycheck. And, of course, if I didn't sell, I didn't eat.

"So to Aleen, that wasn't a job. That sort of shook me a little bit and I saw the humor in the fact that many people couldn't conceive of what I was doing and what a lot of the people I was working with were doing.

"Zig Ziglar joined Holiday Magic the same day I did, in the same office, in the same meeting with Bill Dempsey. So, I was rather quickly in a pond with some heavy hitters. Although 18 years older than I was, Zig was also just beginning in "big money sales," and Holiday Magic is where he hit his stride and took off.

"So that was the pool I was swimming in… while Aleen Harris was working for the government doing something, riding a bus each day to and from work, and her husband was working as a delivery man in a vending machine business. So, to them, $40,000 a month was beyond their comprehension. More importantly, my income didn't necessarily come every Friday. The good news was that, for me, $20,000 might come on a Tuesday, so I didn't even have to wait until Friday!

"My dad said something he had read once. And he told me when I was talking about the Aleens of this world. You know, the people laughing at my goals.

"'They weren't trying to hold you back,' he said. 'They just think your goals are funny because they can't relate to you.' He continued, 'Ben, you will worry less about what people think about you when you realize how infrequently they do.'

"That was a huge step forward for me. I used to worry, 'What is so-and-so going to say?' The truth is, they weren't thinking about me at all unless I was standing in front of them. They weren't aware I was alive when I wasn't there. They were busy doing their own stuff!

"The thing about haters… the world is *not* full of haters. It is full of people who probably don't understand your goals. But once you reach those goals, these people who didn't understand will probably be asking you for a job."

Ben beat his "millionaire due-date" by three years, attaining that goal at the age of 27. Part of the discipline to accomplish such a challenging task was to actually set that goal.

Even before his first year in business Ben had already decided he wanted to make a million dollars. And not an inflation-adjusted million. A million dollars in actual current-value money. He wrote down, "Make a million dollars."

But, at the end of three months he was way off schedule. Halfway through the year he was even further behind. What was he doing wrong?

In later conversations with his friend and mentor, Dr. Napoleon Hill, author of *Think and Grow Rich*, whose most famous quote is "Whatever the mind can see and believe, it can achieve," Ben came to realize whatever the mind manages to see and believe it *can* achieve . . . so long as it is specific, measurable, and attainable

> "I said I want to make a million dollars. I thought back to that conversation with Dr. Hill; not conversations actually, it was a long argument for quite some time before we settled up. 'Okay,' I thought, 'break it down.'
>
> "So instead of making a million dollars a year and discovering on December 1st I'm in deep trouble, I divided it by 365 days and figured out what I had to really make was $2,739.73 a

day. If I did that every day for a year, I would have made a million dollars.

"Another little trick I came to understand was that, like a professional golfer, once you hit a shot, you leave that shot. Good or bad is not important. What is important is where the ball lies now and what you're going to do with it there.

"So, let's say today my goal is to make $2739.73. I round it up to $2,800 because it's easier to remember. My goal is to make $2,800 today.

"If I make $5,600 today, tomorrow morning when I wake up, I don't have a day off. I still have to make $2,800 that day. And the next day, and the next day. I take every day as if it were a championship fight – all by itself. And if I don't make $2,800 today, when I wake up tomorrow, I don't have a $5,600 burden on my head. Like the professional golfer, I concentrate on *this* shot. *Today* I have to make $2,800.

"As you become more successful you come to realize that there are windfalls that come your way to meet your goals.

"For example, I was once hired by a good friend of mine to help him launch a new company in Norway. He paid my speaking fee of $9,500 for each of 10 talks that spread over 11 days. So, that was $95,000.

"On top of that, he bought 20,000+ copies of my books and had them sent to Norway. That amount, with its royalties, was a substantial amount in and of itself.

"And, when my speaking engagements were done, I attended a board of directors meeting the last night I was there. At that meeting I was told I had done a good job and that, as a bonus, they were giving me 3% of the company. This was a publicly traded company on the European stock exchange. My 3% on the day they gave it to me was worth $14 million (US).

"Sometimes you surpass your goals!"

Though Ben had just earned, with his bonus, over a million dollars a day, he was undaunted.

Talking to a friend that night, Ben told him what happened and his friend said, "My God! You don't have to do anything for several years." Ben reminded him, "No, I still have to make $2,800 *tomorrow*."

For Ben, there is a need to keep his goals right in front of him. In this way he overcomes any fear or procrastination. He also is in the habit of writing his plans down. They don't necessarily have to be a goal. He writes down what he is planning to do that day, and then tomorrow, and then the next day, and so on.

He also has next year's calendar already filling up – next year's edition of the same book sitting on his desk where he is writing down activities he intends to be doing a year from now.

As is his morning routine when he comes to the office, the first thing he does before he checks an e-mail or turns on the computer, is to look at his calendar to see what he is supposed to do that day. Such discipline leads to success.

> "So, whenever anyone comes to me with a question on how do you do this, or what do you do about that, I say, 'Learn a success system in whatever situation you're in, and then follow the system – whether you feel like it or not.' Your feelings really aren't terribly important when you're achieving your goals."

It is this discipline that allows Ben to overcome the inevitable roadblocks he faces in the business world. He becomes intent on accomplishing each item on his daily list in the order he has assigned them.

Ben strongly recommends that a person in business listen to Earl Nightingale's "The Strangest Secret." As Ben says, "I listen to it at least once a month. Whenever I get off track a little bit, I go back and listen to it." Nightingale wrote and recorded "The Strangest Secret" in 1956. In that roughly 30-minute presentation, now a video which can be found on YouTube, he defined a successful life.

And at least once a year Ben makes it a point to read "*Think and Grow Rich*" by his old friend Dr. Napoleon Hill. Ben first received the book from an early sales mentor, Bill Dempsey. He uses Hill's words of wisdom to see how he is doing according to his daily lists and life.

Ben also suggests going to the website: hardtofindseminars. com. Run by his good friend Michael Senoff, Ben observes, "It is a great little treasure; where Michael has interviewed hundreds of successful people in various fields." One can easily go on their computer or mobile device, enter a code word that is provided for free and listen to various people. "Me included!" Ben quips. "My presentations are mostly on selling, marketing, and success."

It was during an interview with Michael that Ben shared an "obstacle" that would have crushed lesser men. Ben acknowledged that he had prepared a set answer in case anybody raised their hand and said, "Mr. Gay, were you ever in prison?"

Yes, Ben had been at San Quentin State Prison as a volunteer doing his class called "*People Builders*." He did this for five years. Going into the prison every Friday night at six o'clock, he then taught until six o'clock Saturday morning. In this way, he put 1,000+ people through that self-betterment program.

But, Ben admitted, what someone asking that question of whether he had been in prison might be referring to, no doubt in a snide manner, was his six years, one month, one day and two hours that he spent as a "guest of the federal government in a gated community in southern California." More precisely, Lompoc Federal Prison.

> "That was sort of a little stumble that came upon me from a very successful business.

"The federal government decided they didn't like my business and they raided our office one day and, a few years later, I was indicted. The subsequent trial would last an entire year!

"I knew I was innocent. But, to expedite things, the government offered me a plea-bargain deal of three years incarceration. I was advised that the three years could translate into only a year, no more than two, for 'good behavior.'

"I'm not one to sacrifice my integrity for the easy way out. I told my attorney, 'Let's go to trial.' Who knew that trial would consume an entire year?! Ironically, the trial's length was the amount of time I would have probably done had I taken their plea agreement.

"Unfortunately, what I didn't realize was federal judges are not real fond of having their courtrooms tied up for a year. So, when the jury found me guilty on several of the counts, and I went up for my sentencing, the judge sentenced me to fifteen years!

"At that time the old law required that you do at least one-third, and no more than two-thirds of your sentence. Unless, of course, you stabbed a guard. That meant that I had to do at least five years, but it could be up to ten years! I wound up doing six years, one month, one day and two hours. But, who's counting!

"Now, one could let that get them down. I mean, it's a little stumbling block – being thrown into federal prison for six years. What did I do? I did what I always had done. I had my calendar sent to me from home; I had some copies of "*The Closers*" sent in too.

"From there I went to the warden and got permission to teach sales and marketing classes, even public speaking classes. Eventually, I ran their Educational Department for a couple of years, where I helped hundreds of people get their high school equivalency (GED) diplomas. I taught them how to write; I taught some how to read for the first time. As Michael Senoff said in an interview, 'So, Ben Gay took his show on the road!'

"My point is, I didn't do anything different in prison than I did on the outside. The only difference was I got paid with cans of tuna. Tuna, that's one of the coins of the realm. A copy of "*The Closers*" was four cans of tuna, and so on. After a while it was like I was running a grocery store out of my locker!

"But I did precisely in prison what I was doing before and what I'm doing now. The only difference was, the 'coin of the realm' changed and my sleeping quarters weren't as nice as they are in our home. Everything else was basically the same.

"So, what do you do with a stumbling block? You go back to the systems that have always worked for you. I was walking across the yard one day when the warden saw me. I was on the way to hand out commissary purchases. I ran the regional warehouse the last five years I was there. I was almost like a staff member.

"So anyway, the warden called out to me, 'Mr. Gay!' I turned and said, 'Yes sir. How are you?' He said, 'I'm fine.' I had my folder under my arm. I was going to work. He said, 'Are we ever going to break you?' I said, 'Mr. Craig, I didn't even know you were trying,' and he dropped his head and laughed as he went back in his office.

"Over time I gained approval from the correctional officers. As trust built, I eventually did their taxes, even approved their overtime in the warehouse. If you've ever seen the movie *Shawshank Redemption*, well, I was the Tim Robbins character, Andy Dufresne. You know, the financial genius wrongly imprisoned for a crime he did not commit. Who did all the corrections peoples' taxes and all. It was like that for me as well.

"You see, nothing had changed for me. I had a system that I *knew* worked. I had confidence in myself. What I had going for me was that I didn't go to prison at 18, where I was unprepared for life. I went to prison at 48, when I was successful, fully formed, and knew how to apply those procedures that had worked for me in the past.

"The systems, including setting goals I had used to rise to the top of the ranks in the business world, I used to rise to the top in prison. It was not because of a formal, college education; it was heartfelt determination. If nothing else, I'm persistent.

"And, if truth be told, I made some of the best friends of my life in prison. It was a great experience. How's that for optimism!

"I even met our adopted kid there. I have two stepchildren, and adopted another. He was a young black drug dealer.

"I first met him when he came to prison; he was eighteen. Four or five years ago, he graduated second in his class from San Francisco State Law School. His proud graduation picture sits on our dining room hutch with all our other family members. I wouldn't have met him if I hadn't gone there!"

From this, one can see how Ben meets any obstacle: Head on. Perseverance produces success. And another observation: Success breeds more success. Just ask his adopted son. That is why it is so wise to seek out a mentor (or two) who can help guide you towards that success.

Ben relates how his father taught him that he should listen to people who were successful. His father was his first mentor, especially when it came to personal character growth and personal development in business. As noted, his father put Ben in situations that allowed him to associate with such successful business people as the chairman of the board of Coca Cola, and many other powerful people.

As Ben began to move up through the ranks, he started meeting other successful business people. William Penn Patrick, "Bill," was the owner of Holiday Magic Cosmetics, who Ben came to know as a best friend as he began running Patrick's many companies around the world.

But his contacts were not just from the business world. Bill Patrick actually ran for governor of the State of California against the then famous actor, Ronald Reagan. Reagan, who would not only go on to be governor, but become a two-term President of the United States, was, in Ben's eyes, "a very profound and deep guy; indirectly he taught me a tremendous amount and visited our offices on a couple of occasions seeking Bill's endorsement and our financial donations."

Then there was Ben's jogging buddy, whom he met in his high school days. James H. Rucker, Jr., "Jimmy," was, again in Ben's estimation, the greatest salesman he had ever worked with. As a result, Ben learned a lot about sales from Jimmy. It was part of the reason that Ben rose so rapidly through the ranks.

Earl Nightingale, as noted, author and producer of "The Strangest Secret," became not only the voice of every company Ben Gay ran, he became a close personal friend as well. J. Douglas Edwards, "the best sales trainer of his day," also became a mentor of Ben's. After Edwards died, and at the request of the family, Ben wrote a book in Edward's name from Edwards' seminar recordings, as well as Ben's personal notes from those times.

And, of course, there was Dr. Napoleon Hill, who became Ben's personal mentor and confidante. Dr. Hill's trustworthiness to maintain confidentiality between himself and Ben is legendary. He worked with Ben the last couple of years of his life, never betraying that trust.

Eventually Ben's circle would also include people of faith such as Dr. Norman Vincent Peale and Dr. Robert Schuller, known for the Crystal Cathedral in Orange County California. Men such as Og Mandino worked for Ben in seminars, as well as Dr. Maxwell Maltz. And, as we noted, so did Colonel James Irwin who commanded Apollo 15. Colonel Irwin introduced Ben to the "new pioneers," the fascinating men and women who made up America's astronaut corps.

Not all of his mentors had noble pasts.

> "Sally Stanford had once been a high-priced
> madam in San Francisco. As a businessman,
> I looked at that for what it was: Sally ran a
> unique and successful *business*! That business

sense eventually landed her the political job of mayor of Sausalito, California and ownership of a very successful restaurant in the same town!

"I am not ashamed to say, Sally was a dear friend of mine and one of the wisest people I have ever met... in spite of her background. And local legend has it that the United Nations was formed in her San Francisco "parlor" in 1948. It was where many of the diplomats and dignitaries relaxed in the evenings.

"And, of course, there was my teaching at San Quentin. This was when I was a trainer, not a 'resident.' One of the inmates asked if he could meet me. Because of who it was, he could not come to my classes; I had to go to his cell to meet him. The prisoner's name? Charlie Manson.

"So I went to his cell and spent about nine hours over three different occasions (three hours each time) with convicted mass-murderer, Charlie Manson.

"For safety reasons, although he had a two man cell, he was the only one in it. On the top bunk, which he used for storage, were his personal belongings and a 'bookcase.' Charlie Manson had one book on that shelf – a grand total of *one* book: *"How to Win Friends and*

Influence People" by Dale Carnegie. It was a classic then, and remains one of the classic self-improvement books of all time.

"I said, 'Charlie, that's an interesting book.' He replied, 'It's my bible. It's how I built the Manson family.'"

Understand, Ben would seek knowledge from *any* source placed in his path!

Part of the ability to gain access to these multi-faceted avenues of knowledge is Ben's personality. There is still some of that class clown lurking inside him.

"As I go through my day, working the items off that day's list, I look around at the interesting people I may meet. If someone appears to have something on the ball, I go over and introduce myself to them. 'Hi, I am Ben Gay! Ben Gay, just like the back rub. Don't rub it in!' That gets them laughing and opens the door to turning them into a friend.

"I was reflecting the other day, at age 74, all of my friends are definitely *not* in the graveyard. In fact, I was figuring out that the 'average' age of my many friends is currently about 35-40 years old. Through that youthful input, I've stayed young. And have kept searching out mentors. As they say, 'Out of the mouth of babes.' You can see why I look for possible friends every day, and everywhere I go!

"There was a poem in the flower children era of the 1960s called *Desiderata*. I had it framed and hanging on my office wall for years. It basically said, 'You go your way and I'll go mine. And, if by chance, we meet . . .' It was, you know, just hippie flower-power stuff.

"But in the middle of it was a sentence I have never forgotten: 'Listen to the dull and ignorant. They, too, have their story.' I've learned many things from many people, some whom could barely write their names.

"That is why I know there are always millions of people out there who can teach me useful things that I don't know yet. I continually seek those people out. And try to turn them into friends with my humor."

So Ben Gay III will never stop meeting people. It remains his passion. In his 60-plus years of business and conducting his seminars, he estimates he has shaken the hands of about two and a half million people! About two and a half million people! And he is hoping to add *at least* another million more before he's done!

To accomplish that, he is off to the next seminar – that's where he meets the most people and has the most fun. If you have ever been to one of his meetings, you know he is in heaven wandering up and down the halls talking to people, meeting new folks. Ben just absolutely loves interacting with others!

And he knows only one thing can stop him.

"When the Power Ball lottery in California got up to like a billion dollars a few years ago, my wife, Gigi, went and bought us a ticket. Actually, she does this every week, regardless of the amount. She calls it her 'retirement fund.' I say, 'We already have a better one. Don't worry about it!'

"Anyway, because it got up that high, I think she bought two tickets that week and she said, 'Ben if we win, what are you going to do? What are you going to do differently?' I said, 'Well, if we win, I'm going to call P. Michael Hunt (who is my financial advisor of 50 years) and I'm going to tell him about *his* new financial challenge. Then I'm going to go upstairs to the office, write the next newsletter, and take phone calls.'

"That's what I love doing. People say, 'When are you going to retire?' 'To what?' I say. I'm not digging ditches now. I just do 24 seminars a year, sit around talking to people and, when there isn't anyone to talk to, I write stuff. And I will do all of this until the day I die.

"I had an old friend, Cavett Roberts, a great speaker in his own right. He once said, 'Ben, I hope you get to die on stage.' He said this lovingly because, in fact, he almost did! He had a massive heart attack while speaking at the American Dental Association's yearly convention. They hauled him off on a stretcher and people thought he was dead.

"But, a year later he returned. As he walked on stage he began, 'As I was saying...' Then, he went right back into his stuff.

"Yes, on stage would be a good place to go!"

There is always one question Ben acknowledges should be asked of any successful person. It should, in a few seconds, define them and their accomplishments: *In all of your years of success, what is the one quote that has stuck with you, and from which you still use to this day today?*

"Great question! Let me preface my answer with what I read by Winston Churchill many years ago. And with my lack of formal education, you'll see why I chose it: 'Uneducated people should read books of quotes.'

"What he meant by that, Churchill explained later, was that a famous or successful person can relate, in a short sentence or two, what he or she has learned from years of experience. Or from a deeply intense experience or set of experiences.

"I saw such wisdom in that quote that I have about 25 books containing quotes of one sort or another in my personal library. They are within arm's reach because I use them for references and inspiration. I cannot stress enough: Do not underestimate the value of powerful quotes from interesting and famous and powerful people.

"Now, to my own answer to that question. I will give you *two* quotes. Ed Danforth, who I never met, was head of Ralston Purina, the animal food company. When I read a quote of his, it just jumped off the page at me. He was talking about why some people are successful and some people are not. He said, 'Successful people do what unsuccessful people are not willing to do, because successful people are after pleasing results while unsuccessful people are after pleasing methods.'

"That really describes me in my earliest Holiday Magic Cosmetics days. Successful people memorized the scripts, which I initially didn't, because successful people were after successful results. The reason I didn't was because I was after pleasing methods. So, I was predictably unsuccessful.

"The second quote deals with managing. And it really turned my business life around. It was in William Penn Patrick's office, not long after I had been made president of the Holliday Magic Cosmetics. Looking back, I realize how young and inexperienced I was in business management.

"I was whining to Bill about a man I had hired. I was trying to turn his life around, but it wasn't working. Bill cut me off, 'Benjamin, I really want to apologize to you. I didn't explain your job properly when I made you president of the company. I did not ask you to go out and purposefully change lives. I should have made it clear that you were not to drag people out of the gutter, hose them off, and turn them into successes so you could point them out to show how good you were in changing their lives.'

"With that as background, here's the quote: 'People are going to do what they've always done which, in most cases unfortunately, is nothing.'

"Bill went on to say, 'I don't want you to go find people and change lives. In the work we do, and not by accident, you'll be astounded at how many lives you're going to positively affect anyway.

"'When you're putting people on payroll, this is not the Salvation Army. What I want you to do is go find people who are *already* successfully doing what we want done… and then have them come over here and do it for *us*!

"'And the best place to start, if it exists, is to find a mailing list of former Eagle Scouts – and then hire all of them!' "

Now into his seventh decade of commissioned selling, what closing advice would the Ben Gay of today offer Ben Gay of his youth?

> "I would take 'it' more seriously, and sooner than I actually did. 'It' can be business; 'it' can be personal growth; 'it' can be learning and, in my case, the skills of being a Professional Salesperson, and so on. But I would take 'it' more seriously *sooner*.

> "In my senior year in high school I was voted the Funniest and Wittiest in our graduating class. In reality, that's like being voted Most Likely to Fail. That title would have changed, positively changed, if I had taken 'it' more seriously and sooner. And 'it' at that time was learning; that's what we are in school for!

> "One of the drawbacks of being the funny guy was that I could go gliding through life. I could get in a tight situation and quip my way out of it. I was hard to hate (though some people managed to break through and do it anyway) because I could have you laughing pretty fast.

> "Because I could laugh my way into or out of almost any situation, I didn't take 'it' seriously enough and quick enough. I took this attitude into my early career in selling and it cost me a lot of time – almost my entire career.

"Some people say, 'Well, what difference does that really make? You are still successful.' But, in the grand total, it makes a big difference... to me.

"I'm 74 years old. I wish I had been this smart at 24, 34, 44, 54 or even 64. And I could have been if only I had taken 'it' more seriously right from the start.

"So this is the lesson I would like to pass along to the young Ben Gay. And to the up-and-coming 'young Bens' of today."

As one can see, all of these insights are why Ben Gay III has had a long, successful, and profitable *life*!

Selected Sources

BOOKS

Brown, Les. *Laws of Success 12 Laws That Turn Dreams Into Reality*. Germantown, Maryland: Lurn Publishing, 2016.

Canfield, Jack, with Janet Switzer. *The Success Principles: How to Get from Where You Are to Where You Want to Be*. New York: Harper, 2005.

Colvin, Elain Wright, and Elaine Creasman. *Treasury of God's Virtues*. Lincolnwood, Illinois: Publications International, 1999.

Dungy, Tony, with Nathan Whitaker. *The Mentor Leader: Secrets to Building People and Teams that Wi Consistently*. Carol Stream, Illinois: Tyndale House Publishers, Inc., 2010.

Hickman, Gill Robinson, ed. *Leading Organizations: Perspectives for a New Era*. Thousand Oaks, California: Sage Publications, 1998.

Hill, Napoleon. *Think and Grow Rich Action Pack*. New York: Penguin Books, 1972.

Kouzes, James M., and Barry Z. Posner. *Credibility: How Leaders Gain and Lose It, Why People Demand It*. Jossey-Bass Management Series. San Francisco, California: Jossey-Bass, Inc. Publishers, 1993.

Rae, Scott B. *Moral Choices: An Introduction to Ethics.* 2d ed. Grand Rapids, Michigan: Zondervan Publishing House, 1995, 2000.

Reddy, W. Brendan, PhD. *Intervention Skills: Process Consultation for Small Groups and Teams.* San Francisco, California: Jossey-Bass/Pfeiffer, 1994.

Ulrich, Dave, Jack Zenger, and Norm Smallwood. Results-Based Leadership. Boston: Harvard Business School Press, 1999.

INTERVIEWS

Cayer, Chris. Telephone interview with Sean P. McCullough, November 6, 2016; transcribed by Gloria Hass before March 16, 2017. Recording and transcript in McCullough Collection, Havertown, Pennsylvania.

Etheridge, Lane. Telephone interview with Sean P. McCullough, October 17, 2016; transcribed by Gloria Hass before July 12, 2017. Recording and transcript in McCullough Collection, Havertown, Pennsylvania.

Frank, Stephanie. Telephone interview with Sean P. McCullough, November 20, 2016; transcribed by Gloria Hass before February 28, 2017. Recording and transcript in McCullough Collection, Havertown, Pennsylvania.

Gay III, Ben. Telephone interview with Sean P. McCullough, November 7, 2016; transcribed by Gloria Hass before January 21, 2017. Recording and transcript in McCullough Collection, Havertown, Pennsylvania.

Holmes, Bob. Telephone interview with Sean P. McCullough, March 3, 2017; transcribed by Gloria Hass before July 3, 2017. Recording and transcript in McCullough Collection, Havertown, Pennsylvania.

Hoyt, Paul. Telephone interview with Sean P. McCullough, December 12, 2016; transcribed by Gloria Hass before April 3, 2017. Recording and transcript in McCullough Collection, Havertown, Pennsylvania.

Lofholm, Eric. Telephone interview with Sean P. McCullough, December 19, 2016; transcribed by Gloria Hass before April 19, 2017. Recording and transcript in McCullough Collection, Havertown, Pennsylvania.

MacArthur, Ken. Telephone interview with Sean P. McCullough, March 3, 2017; transcribed by Gloria Hass before May 11, 2017. Recording and transcript in McCullough Collection, Havertown, Pennsylvania.

McGee, Dr. Jeff. Telephone interview with Sean P. McCullough, March 4, 2017; transcribed by Gloria Hass before April 26, 2017. Recording and transcript in McCullough Collection, Havertown, Pennsylvania.

Moreleand, Dr. Will. Telephone interview with Sean P. McCullough, November 7, 2016; transcribed by Gloria Hass before March 1, 2017. Recording and transcript in McCullough Collection, Havertown, Pennsylvania.

Peterson, Jessica. Telephone interview with Sean P. McCullough, October 31, 2016; transcribed by Gloria Hass before March 8, 2017. Recording and transcript in McCullough Collection, Havertown, Pennsylvania.

Rochon, Ken. Telephone interview with Sean P. McCullough, March 2, 2017; transcribed by Gloria Hass before June 6, 2017. Recording and transcript in McCullough Collection, Havertown, Pennsylvania.

Salem, Chris. Telephone interview with Sean P. McCullough, October 23, 2016; transcribed by Gloria Hass before March 27, 2017. Recording and transcript in McCullough Collection, Havertown, Pennsylvania.

Schwartz, Dr. Len. Telephone interview with Sean P. McCullough, November 14, 2016; transcribed by Gloria Hass before May 11, 2017. Recording and transcript in McCullough Collection, Havertown, Pennsylvania.

Salomon, Robert "Bob," interview with Rick Young, July 4, 2017.

Vaughn, Jim. Telephone interview with Sean P. McCullough, November 6, 2016; transcribed by Gloria Hass before February 16, 2017. Recording and transcript in McCullough Collection, Havertown, Pennsylvania.

Williams, Coach Andre M. Telephone interview with Sean P. McCullough, November 6, 2016; transcribed by Gloria Hass before May 10, 2017. Recording and transcript in McCullough Collection, Havertown, Pennsylvania.

ABOUT THE AUTHORS

Sean P. McCullough is a successful entrepreneur with over 25-years' experience in owning and operating his own businesses. He caught the entrepreneurial bug in 5th grade selling Jolly Ranchers to his fellow students. After graduating high school Sean started his first successful business, Helping Hands Cleaning & Maintenance and built that company to a multiple 6-figure enterprise before entering the real estate and insurance industries. He is the founder and director of Young Eagle Entrepreneurs, a leadership and business development program specifically designed for graduating high school seniors, college age students, and young adults interested in becoming entrepreneurs in their own chosen businesses. He was the captain of his high school football and wrestling teams, as well as captain of his university golf team. Sean holds a Bachelor of Arts in Education from Neumann University.

Rick Young, PhD, is a combat veteran of the Vietnam War serving there from May 1968 until December 1969. He is a retired senior special agent with over 28 years in federal law enforcement. Rick currently writes as a second profession and is the author of *Combat Police Police: U.S. Army Military Police in Vietnam*; *Matters of Consequence: Critical Eschatological Issues Impacting Endtime Preparation* (his doctoral dissertation);

co-author with Michael E. Bolyog of the *Aiden's Cauldron Trilogy* including the books *Aiden's Cauldron*, *Summoner's InnsKeep*, and *BlackFriar's End*; and co-author with Bob Salomon of the children's picture book *Beyond The Laces*. Rick's Masters is in Organizational Leadership from Cairn University (then, Philadelphia Biblical University) and his doctorate in Eschatology is from Luder-Wycliffe Seminary.

Printed in the United States
By Bookmasters